These Came Back

These Came Back

by Richard Webb

HAWTHORN BOOKS, INC.
PUBLISHERS / *New York*

THESE CAME BACK

Copyright © 1974 by Richard Webb. Copyright under International and Pan-American Copyright Conventions. All rights reserved, including the right to reproduce this book or portions thereof in any form, except for the inclusion of brief quotations in a review. All inquiries should be addressed to Hawthorn Books, Inc., 260 Madison Avenue, New York, New York 10016. This book was manufactured in the United States of America and published simultaneously in Canada by Prentice-Hall of Canada, Limited, 1870 Birchmount Road, Scarborough, Ontario.

Library of Congress Catalog Card Number: 73–21324
ISBN: 0–8015–7580–X

1 2 3 4 5 6 7 8 9 10

To my wife, Florence.
We've known each other
in many lifetimes.

CONTENTS

Introduction by Dr. Freda Morris ... ix

Part I The Return-Trip Ticket

   1 A Pattern of Prophecy and Coincidence ... 3
   2 Types of Recall ... 16
   3 We've Known Each Other in Many Lifetimes ... 38
   4 A Past and Present Life Reading ... 48

Part II Dreams, Waking and Sleeping

   5 I Think I Was Suffocated ... 59
   6 His Transitional Lifetime ... 65
   7 What Was It? ... 72
   8 Kiyo ... 75
   9 They Called Me *Gracias a Dios* ... 83

Part III Time-Tripping and Projection

   10 He Lived in the Fourth and Nineteenth Centuries ... 91
   11 Pictures in My Eyes ... 110
   12 I Was Waiting to Be Born Again ... 116
   13 Reincarnation and Continuing Life ... 123
   14 Dreaming True ... 130
   15 I Can't Stay Long ... 139
   16 This Time I Am an Indian ... 146

Part IV Trance and Spirit Communication

17 I Was a Primitive Man — 153
18 Just Call Me Ulysses — 163

Afterword — 175
Bibliography — 181
Index — 183

INTRODUCTION

Greater clarity is often reached by turning the standard way of looking at something upside down. Science has an aversion to purpose. Someone once described the scientist as a man who is dedicated to the purpose of proving that neither he nor anyone else has any purpose. Let's pretend that everything has the purpose of realizing its potential and see where this leads us with regard to the credibility of reincarnation.

We shall begin by reviewing the qualities of light, then note how matter originated, follow the development of the universe, and end by considering the evidence for and the value of the reincarnation hypothesis.

Reasoning backward from our human state, in which we clearly feel our purposefulness, we will return to as near the beginning as we can conceptualize and assume that we were once light with the purpose of realizing our potential.

Paradigm for Purposive Change

As light, we were indivisible, unpredictable, and dimensionless quanta of action—photons. We were bounded only by a maximum speed, at which we constantly moved, 186,000 miles per second. At this speed time stands still. Hence, we existed outside time.

We had tremendous energy and great freedom but we lacked experience. We were like an energetic child who is free to run all over the place but doesn't know where to go or what to do. Moved by our purpose of realizing our potential, we sought experience. We bound together in just the right way, and two photons became a nuclear particle. We learned the value of binding together, came into time, and learned about substance.

We nuclear particles made ourselves into atoms and learned about form and identity, how it feels to be different from one another. Then as atoms we combined, created molecules, and learned about stability, immobility, solidarity, and how to combine and combine and combine. In the process of all these steps, energy levels were constantly lowered. The one billion electron volts that the photon started with were reduced to one twenty-fifth of an electron volt in the average molecule at room temperature.

It just so happens that life is possible at this energy level. As molecules, we hooked up in more and more complex chains and loops and bundles until we produced the giant molecules of DNA and RNA and made possible the development of cells.

By this time we had learned enough about the laws governing binding, attraction, and combination so that we could transcend these laws and make use of them. And so a drastic change occurred. Whereas we had been giving up freedom and energy with every step in our growth, this time the process was reversed.

A miracle occurred! We became living plants, able to grow down into the earth and up toward the sun and thus become huge; to store energy by making our own food with the help of light; and to produce progeny. Complex organization was an important lesson we learned, and from knowing it we were able to cover Earth (and probably many other planets, too).

After a few eons of rootedness we decided we wanted to learn about mobility and to experiment with new shapes, sizes, and activities. We gave up making our own food and became animals, capable of moving about at our own volition. We experimented with many strange body shapes and developed all kinds of skills. We learned to fly, walk, swim, swing, batter, cut, saw, make music, see, hear, run, fight, build homes, mate, care for our young—and much, much more.

After evolving an incredible array of unbelievable bodies

and reaching the limits of biological mobility, we realized that there were other kinds of things to learn, and so became human. We kept an animal body but chose from among the many styles the one that was most capable of building tools. We got our ideas for tools from the other bodies we had lived in. Instead of keeping wings for flying, we made airplanes. Instead of keeping beaver teeth for chewing down trees, we invented the saw. Instead of a woodpecker bill, we made a drill. Instead of an elephant trunk to lift with, we made a hoist. Instead of keeping a long tail, we developed rope.

Since we became humans, our bodies have changed very little. There was no point in developing different kinds of bodies to fulfill the needs we so ably met with our inventions. Obviously, our mobility lesson has been learned and there is a new lesson we are mastering as humans. Just what, is not clear. At this point in our theorizing we begin to catch up with ourselves. Perhaps we can get some ideas about where we are going by taking another look at where we've been.

Each time we learned a new lesson we did a brief review of past lessons and a sneak preview of the lessons yet to be learned. For example, when we first learned identity by becoming atoms, we got a little touch of combination, growth, and mobility. Later we learned these lessons well as molecules, plants, and animals. But as each of these things we still went through all the lessons again. Plants started as one cell and ended as flowers; animals, building on the lessons of plants, still began as one cell and reiterated the lessons of binding together, developing identity, combining many cells, and so on.

We somehow became people, learned to band together in primitive tribes, developed a sense of identity, and put two and two together, that is, combined observations and thus developed objective thought. A few of us (the creative geniuses) have been able to store our energy in great works or new civilizations. This is comparable to the change that came with the development of plant life—that is, energy was no longer wasted but saved.

Most of us aren't geniuses, but we are able to put two and two together. This means that in the total scheme of things we are as far along as the molecules are in their realm and have yet to learn how to stop wasting energy. In terms of animal evolution we are about as advanced as the clam.*

This state of affairs can be seen as quite encouraging. It means that great opportunity lies ahead of us. How can we best make use of the knowledge we have gained, gain new knowledge at a maximum rate, and facilitate the growth of wisdom?

We have always repeated our lessons over and over in order to learn them thoroughly. Undoubtedly we must repeat our experiences as people over and over, too. Let's look at the empirical evidence. After that let's consider how the study of past lives can make the current life more effective in the realization of one's potential, both in the current life and in those yet to come.

Remembrance of Things Past

As four-year-old William wandered into the bedroom where his mother was looking through her jewelry box, he spied a gold watch lying on the bed, a watch that had been locked in the jewelry box since before he was born and had never been mentioned in his presence.

"Mama, that's my watch!" he cried excitedly, grabbed the watch, and clung to it tenaciously. He repeated his claim over and over, and was willing to return the watch to the box only when his mother convinced him that she would store it there for him.

This occurred in 1954. William is now a young man and still claims the watch for his own. How he came to have this watch is a strange and convincing story.

William's grandfather was a fishing boat captain in Alaska, and like many people in that area he looked favorably on the idea of reincarnation. In 1949 he told his favorite son and daughter-in-law that he intended to be reborn as their son.

"And you will recognize me because I will have birthmarks

---

* The author is indebted to Arthur Young, founder of the Institute for the Study of Consciousness, for many of the ideas presented here.

like the ones I now have," he said, referring to the round marks on his left shoulder and forearm. A little while later he gave them his gold watch and said, "I'll come back. Keep this watch for me. I will return as your son and claim it."

Shortly after this he was killed in a boating accident. About nine months later his daughter-in-law gave birth to William, who bore round birthmarks on his left shoulder and forearm. In addition, when he learned to walk he manifested a peculiar limp like the limp his grandfather had had.

When he was four, William excitedly ran into the house to report that he had seen his "sister" pass by. He was referring to his grandfather's sister. His statement and his excitement were totally unexplainable unless she *was* his sister whom he had missed since the boating accident five years earlier.

William's understanding of boats and the bay was uncanny, and without any previous experience he could point out the best places to fish.*

This case is typical of hundreds carefully documented by a cautious investigator, Dr. Ian Stevenson, former chief psychiatrist at the University of Virginia Medical School and now head of the Division of Parapsychology.

In some cases of this nature the young child is able to remember where he hid something during his past life and to find the object when he has the opportunity to go to the place in question.**

Another startling phenomenon that is difficult to explain without the reincarnation hypothesis involves the remarkable talents of child prodigies. The incredible accomplishments of the boy Mozart are well known. Less familiar is Carol Gallacher of Glasgow, Scotland. If she was a Frenchman in previous life, it is not so surprising to find her singing the "Marseillaise" in French at the age of two. If she studied the books in another life, her ability to read and understand *Gulliver's Travels* and *Vanity Fair* at the age of four or Plato's *Republic*

---

* Ian Stevenson, *Twenty Cases Suggestive of Reincarnation* (New York: American Society for Psychical Research, 1966).
** See the case of Shanti Devi in C. Ducasse, *The Belief in a Life After Death* (Thomas, 1961), pp. 245–247.

and More's *Utopia* at seven would be more understandable.*

Reports and research on out-of-the-body experience aid the reincarnation hypothesis by suggesting there may be a thinking, feeling something that can exist apart from the body. There are innumerable reports of out-of-the-body experiences in which a person discovers things he should not know since his body is sleeping somewhere else. In some of these experiences the person is able to create a physical effect to establish his existence apart from his body.

Rev. Louis Gittner, who starred in the children's movie series "Our Gang" as the little fat boy, Spanky, has experienced being out of his body regularly since childhood. He would go walking on roof tops at night for fun. One night he met his father there, equally disembodied. The next day at the breakfast table they confirmed the meeting and discussed their mutual interest in out-of-the-body travel for the first time.

Gittner continued his interest as an adult, and after many years of effort he developed the ability to ring a small bell when out of his body. He has several of his friends keep such a bell by their beds so he can let them know when he has made an out-of-the-body visit.**

Because of the conditions of observation and the information retrieved the following case is impressive.

A young woman claimed to have spontaneous out-of-the-body experiences often when she was asleep and to be able to look down on herself from above. She served as a research subject for a week at the dream laboratory at the University of California at Davis. The investigators put a five-digit number on a shelf above her bed and attached short EEG (electro-encephalograph) electrodes to her head so she could not climb up to see the numbers without disrupting the continuous recording of her brain waves.

* G. Hodson, *Reincarnation, Fact or Fallacy?* (Theosophical Publishing House, 1967).
** Lecture by Gittner at Palo Alto, 1972.

One time during the week she slept there she had an out-of-the-body experience and was able to see the numbers. The next morning she reported all five digits in correct order.*

The evidence for communication with people after death, hauntings, and poltergeist phenomena all support the idea that we exist in some viable form between times of manifesting in substance. This literature is fascinating and overwhelming but would take us far afield. Rather than pursue it here, let's turn our attention to the value of the study of reincarnation.

Effect of Belief in Reincarnation

I saw one of the most startling examples of the potent effect of a newly developed interest in reincarnation in a thirty-year-old Los Angeles woman. She felt she had wasted her life in a resentful overinvolvement with her parents. Several times a week she drove through the city to visit her parents' suburban home, where she spent all her spare time doing them unnecessary and unappreciated favors and listening to them belittle her.

She had no significant friendships and no intellectual interests, took no pleasure in cultural pursuits, had no involvement in civic affairs, no hobbies. She worked at a boring, poorly paid job and lived alone in a run-down apartment house.

An overheard conversation about reincarnation piqued the interest of her usually preoccupied mind. She began to read about it and within a few weeks had written the following statements:

> 1. I chose to be incarnated as my parents' child because I needed the atmosphere they provided in which to work out several important lessons.
> 2. I cannot blame them for any effect they have had on me.

* C. Tart, "A Psychophysiological Study of Out-of-the-Body," *Journal of the American Society for Psychical Research* 62 (1966), pp. 3–27.

3. I have learned about anger, resentment, and attachment, and am now able to overcome these feelings and go on to new lessons.

For me, as a psychologist used to working in deep, intensive psychotherapy in which all manner of repressed undercurrents usually have to be rechanneled in order for the person to change, it was quite startling when she completely revamped her life.

She quickly tapered off her commitments to her parents and became involved in painting, horseback riding, and helping children with reading difficulties, to name but three of the growing list of her intense interests. She enjoyed her rare visits with her parents and didn't miss them in between. She changed her job, residence, personality, and appearance. She made many close friends and was soon deeply in love.

This recovery from a severe neurosis seemed to come from an intellectual consideration of the reincarnation hypothesis, an amazingly simple cure.

Effect of Hypnotic Recall of Past Lives

More frequently such extensive benefit comes from a rearrangement of psychic forces at a deeper level. In one of my patients an apparently permanent cure of a severe asthmatic condition occurred as a result of a past life memory. This middle-aged woman had been bothered by asthma all her life. An interest in reincarnation prompted her to seek hypnotic help to recapture memories of a past life in an effort to find the cause, and hopefully a cure, for her asthma.

During the hypnotic session she vividly experienced a life in which she was spurned by her lover. A very strong pride prevented her from expressing her hurt, and she never shed a tear over the lost love. But as she reexperienced the pain she cried and sobbed deeply.

Later, after she had come back from the past life but while still in the hypnotic state, she said that the tears and sobs she had squelched in that life had been expressing themselves in this life in the form of asthma attacks. She told how she had overcome prideful feelings as a young woman in her current life, and pointed out that as a result she was able to shed the bitter tears she had just released. In piecing together the two lives, she somehow shifted her psychic economy so that asthma was no longer necessary. She hasn't had an attack for over five years.

I have worked with many people this way but have had varying degrees of conviction that they were remembering actual past lives. Some were firm believers; others, open-minded; a few, skeptics. It did not seem to matter whether they were ignorant or knowledgeable, sophisticated or naive. I suspect that the emotional impact of vividly experiencing oneself as another person, in another time, having strange experiences and reacting to them in unfamiliar ways, shakes free some psychic energy that can then be used to relate the new material to current problems and ways of coping.

I found this technique especially useful in dealing with emotional blocks. It seems that people are often able to deal with a problem if they can get some distance from it by converting it to a different form, at a different time, and themselves to a different life.

An example was a woman who could not deal with and overcome her own weakness and lack of courage in the face of a domineering husband who was making a nervous wreck of their son with excessive demands, unreasonable punishments, and inconsistent rules. In a past life regression she was a boy with a weak mother and a domineering father. Speaking as the boy, she focused on the relationship with the father and worked it out satisfactorily. She ignored the mother's role except to describe it in detail. The description was an accurate and penetrating analysis of herself in relation to her husband and son.

The woman came out of the hypnotic state with full memory of all that had happened but without apparent realization that it was in any way related to her present situation. Instead, she tried to tie it in with her relationship with her own father.

She went home feeling very good, stood up to her husband, insisted that he take the pressure off the boy, stuck by her guns, and solved the problems with her son. Apparently as a result of this new way of dealing with her husband the intensity and quality of their relationship increased and their marriage improved.

She had a lack of credibility in the presentation of her past life experience, and my feeling was that she had not really lived that life. I did not think she was consciously making it up; she herself might have had complete faith in its validity. As was shown by later events, any lack of validity did not hinder the experience's effectiveness in helping her with her current problems.

In retrospect, after experiencing my own past lives, I feel certain that much comes from fantasy rather than memory. Nevertheless the memories, fantasized or not, have contributed to my self-understanding in a helpful way.

Although the validity of certain past life memories has been established to my satisfaction by Stevenson and others, Stevenson's work also shows that errors occur in the memories of even the most reliable of the children he has studied. As a general rule, past life memories fade rapidly in childhood and early adolescence.

Adults struggling to recall are going to be lucky to have any validity at all. I suspect that the psychological aspects of the memories are accurate. Perhaps the location, the time, the events, the description of the persons, is partly, mostly, or all fantasy. But the types of problems, the kinds of solutions, the struggles, the feelings, and the ways of coping can still reflect the person as he was in a past life.

I have had patients who spent considerable time and energy trying to validate some past life memory. With rare exceptions I see this as wasted effort. Real trouble can occur if the person tries to convince others and becomes upset at not being taken seriously.

Reincarnation is not the standard belief of the Western world, and those with an interest in it are bound to meet with rebuff occasionally. In fact, America and Europe have been described as that small portion of the globe where reincarnation is not accepted.

I recommend that you, the reader, study the literature to the extent of your interest; pursue the evidence of your own past lives through contemplation, meditation, hypnosis, and self-hypnosis as you choose; and enjoy and use whatever results.

This book follows the twistings, turnings, and intermingling of different people's lives as they reveal subtle events that suggest the drama of reincarnations spent together. It gives numerous examples of various kinds of evidence that could easily be overlooked.

By becoming alert and sensitive to such evidence in our own and our friends' lives, we can appreciably increase our understanding of our relationships with others. Such investigations may completely reorient us as to the best approach to our own development.

Perhaps by turning our view of ourselves upside down we may suddenly gain some clarity that will save us a few million repetitions of some mistake and will speed us on our way toward illumination (again, light). By turning ourselves upside down over and over, perhaps we can tumble on our way toward becoming more noble, virtuous, knowledgeable, wise, moral, ethical, happy, joyous beings.

> Freda Morris, Ph.D.
> Center for the Unexplained
> Berkeley, California

PART I
The Return-Trip Ticket

1

A Pattern of Prophecy and Coincidence

The publication of this book is the culmination of what can only be a highly provocative chain of coincidences. The Jungian word for this phenomenon is synchronicity. The events involved cover a period of the last four years but really commenced almost nineteen years ago with a man who has been deceased for eighteen years and has worked with me from the other side. There have been a total of five people involved in the coincidences. Though we've been separated by great distances, it doesn't appear to have mattered.

The initial coincidence began in 1954, when I was starring in the television series "Captain Midnight" for CBS television. The stunt double for my sidekick, Ikky Mudd (Sidney Melton), was a fellow named Louis—Louie for short. I was very fond of Louie; we had a lot of laughs during the filming at Columbia Ranch in the San Fernando Valley. When our series took a two-week break in 1955, Louie was employed by Warner Brothers to do a fight scene aboard a boat in the San Francisco harbor. During the scene Louie misjudged, went over backward, and hit his head on a sharp projection.

He was in a coma for a week and then died. His death saddened me very much. From time to time, over the years, I would remember Louie.

Although my interest in and study of psychic phenomena began in 1965, it wasn't until 1968 that I visited my very first medium. (Some call them sensitives or psychics.) During that session I was told there was someone present from the other side. What that entity said through the meduim was, "I am Louis. I worked with you at the studio. You were very friendly. I fell; I hit my head." For a moment it shook me; I couldn't remember a Louis. Then I replied that I'd known a Louie. The answer came through the medium, "Yes, I am Louie. I worked with you at the studio."

The medium had only been in the San Fernando Valley for five years, knew nothing about me, was not in show business, and my appointment had been set up with her about three days in advance, over the phone. I did not feel there was a likelihood of any cheating on her part. I had not mentioned the name Louie to her before or during the session prior to his coming through, nor had I been thinking of his name.

Over the next few months I returned for more sessions with Louie. I'd ask questions of him, and the answers would come through the medium. Much of the information had to be checked out. One time my wife and I drove over two hundred miles to check out some names I inquired about and found he'd been correct, right down to the last jot and tittle.

At that particular sitting I'd asked Louie who owned an old, abandoned mine high on a hill near where I was "gophering"—prospecting for silver. The answer, through the medium, came immediately: "Adams and Becker." Further questioning could elicit no additional information. I had the exact location of that mine but had never been able to find any evidence of a name, not even an initial. It intrigued me so much that my wife and I drove to Independence, California, the Inyo County seat, to check it out. After two hours of culling through massive mining claim registration books, there at the head of one page was the name Adams, C. L., the name of the mine, and its location, which checked out with my map coordinates. The year was 1901. There was no mention of Becker. Some weeks later, in a sitting with the medium, I shot the question at Louie from left field: "Whatever happened to Becker?" Again, the answer was immediate: "Becker was Adams' partner. He died."

In April of 1969 I was doing a role in a movie being made in Dallas, Texas. A medium there gave me a sitting, during which she contacted Louie. Through her, he said that within six months, "You will go to Mexico to make a movie; the movie will not be made; you will be paid." At the time of the sitting there had been no offers for me to go to Mexico. Six months later I was hired to make a movie in Mexico. The company went down for eighteen days; the movie was not made; I was paid and returned to Los Angeles.

Two months after that sitting in Dallas I was in New Orleans and visited a woman clairvoyant. At that sitting Louie came through her, telling me where I'd been, what I'd been doing. He then said, "You will return to the West. You will write a book. You will think you are writing it. I will be helping you." A few months later, in September of 1969, I sat down and began writing up some ghost stories I'd collected over the years which my wife and friends had insisted should be compiled into a book. Many of the stories had been obtained from people in the Sierra Nevada and the Mojave Desert.

During the writing of that manuscript I was introduced to Dr. Freda Morris, at that time associate professor at the Neuropsychiatric Institute of the University of California at Los Angeles. Dr. Morris gave me the names of a number of people whom she'd checked out for their ghostly materializations or manifestations. Most of the people contacted allowed me to use their stories. Also, at the prompting of Dr. Morris, I joined the Southern California Society for Psychical Research, in Beverly Hills, and became familiar with a new magazine called *Psychic,* published in San Francisco. Upon completion of the manuscript, I sent it to my literary agent in New York. Two weeks later I received a call from the Nash

Publishing Company in Los Angeles; *Great Ghosts of the West* was published by Nash in 1971.

In the spring of 1972, after doing research on the history of stigmata, I wrote an article on the subject. Dr. Morris gave me the address of Alan Vaughan, who was at that time the eastern editor for *Psychic* magazine. I sent Alan the article and he replied that he was interested in publishing it. On April 4, 1972, I received a tape cassette from Alan. He explained that the taping was the result of a reading by a sensitive he was working with by the name of James Neyland. James at that time was an editor with the Macmillan Company in New York. Alan had placed my "Stigmata" article in a plain, unmarked envelope and had given it to James at a psychometry * experiment he was conducting.

The impressions James had picked up from holding the envelope were recorded on the tape. What James correctly picked up about the subject matter and me are quite startling. I've placed the key words (the hits) in italics.

ALAN: Just say what comes into your mind, either about your impression of the author or the subject matter.

JAMES: Well . . . I see a man in his late forties, a man who likes to smile. I feel he is involved with education—not *religious* but *spiritual* education. I think he has *two daughters*. I seem to see him in a western state; it could be *California*. For some reason I get an old Clifton *Webb* movie . . . .

ALAN: Any more associations?

JAMES: Uh . . . there is a *great warmth* about him; he greets people *smilingly,* with a lot of warmth.

ALAN: See if you can pick up something about the manuscript.

JAMES: I'm so familiar with manuscripts I might not get anything.

ALAN: Just say what comes into your mind.

JAMES: I just got an impression of an ape, or gorilla, or something . . . [Christ, with arms outstretched on the cross?] I don't get the writer's *passion* with people that he has in the

---

* Psychometry is the faculty of divining knowledge about an object, or about a person connected with it, through contact with the object.

manuscript. I get the words "in whatever form." I get the image of a wooden gavel, a wooden *hammer*. I get the feeling there is a lot of *philosophy* in this manuscript, not so much religion but philosophy.

ALAN: Can you zero in on the topic of the manuscript—associations?

JAMES: Associations? I'm getting a noose and something like an *oak leaf* . . . an *oak leaf* thing like *Caesar* wore, like a necklace. I'm new at this; it's only the second time I've tried it. Okay, I get a *manger*.

ALAN: What is the association with a manger?

JAMES: Well, of course, *Christmas*. And a *donkey,* a *blue light*.

ALAN: How do you mean, "a blue light"?

JAMES: A *star*—the *star of Bethlehem,* the kind of night you get when there is a very strong moonlight, a very blue light, a wooded setting at night. There are very strong *emotional* vibrations. I can't tell whether it is happiness or *great agony*. I think I'd better stop now.

On April 21, 1972, Alan, himself a psychic sensitive, wrote me that he had a "definite feeling that you and James Neyland are destined to work together on some professional endeavor, very soon."

That psychometry reading by James started a correspondence between us. By that time James had become senior editor at Hawthorn Books in New York. I'd never submitted anything to him in his official capacity, but Alan had told him of a book manuscript I'd written and James asked my New York literary agent to send it to him. He decided not to publish that manuscript, but our correspondence continued.

In a letter to James in July 1973 I mentioned that another manuscript I'd written was being published by a Los Angeles company. Within a month that company went out of business, the manuscript was returned to me, and James asked me to send it to him. After reading it and consulting with the publisher, James called me (just prior to my birthday, when important things always seem to happen) in September 1973 and informed me that *These Came Back* had been accepted.

James also inquired if I knew anyone in the field of parapsychology who would write an introduction for the book. I immediately wrote to Dr. Freda Morris, asking if she would consider doing it. What I didn't know at the time was that Dr. Morris was on her way to New York and she wouldn't receive my letter until after her return. Dr. Morris had prepared a book manuscript of her own, so while she was in New York she looked in the Yellow Pages for the name of a publisher. There are well over one hundred listed. She picked two names; one was Hawthorn. She called the company and was put through to James Neyland, who invited her to the office to discuss her project. James wrote me later that while she was in the office her name kept ringing a bell. He finally asked her if she knew me. Of course she did; the association was connected. James did not know I'd written Dr. Morris about the introduction. Thank you, Dr. Morris. May your Center for the Unexplained help extend the borders of knowledge and understanding of the parapsychic.

People are constantly experiencing chains of synchronistic coincidences. I thought the foregoing was of sufficient interest to include here. You are reading a book brought about by just such a chain. It didn't merely happen by chance. Somehow, it was meant to be.

My wife, Florence, and other astrologers have done comparison readings of my chart with the charts of the above individuals, and in every instance they have found an unusual compatibility; synchronistic aspects that quite possibly are holdovers from a former life during which we knew one another, either individually or collectively— perhaps we worked together.

When astrologers compare Florence's chart with mine, they invariably say, "You've known each other in *many* lifetimes." And that is how we feel, too. That is also true regarding a comparison reading of my chart with that of James Neyland. One point of Karmic reference between us is quite possibly during the period 1804-1869, in and around the eastern seaboard states of the United States. From what has been presently ascertained in the readings, I was in a position during that lifetime to help James (his name wasn't James then, mine wasn't Richard) and he is returning the favor to me in this lifetime. And Alan Vaughan had picked up that there would be an association between us "on some professional endeavor, very soon."

My own personal "bag" in this life consists of two major factors: learning not to commit suicide when I feel (or am) rejected, and learning spirituality. So it really raised my hair the first time I visited an astrologist of some note and was told that according to my natal chart I had committed suicide in a former life and came into this life to learn not to commit suicide. Additionally, the astrologer reported that in 1960, my chart indicated a fatal aspect for me—as if I died but had a spiritual rebirth that I have been trying to live since that time. Both were hits.

How often have you thought, "I know you," upon meeting someone for the first time? You could be right. Maybe you haven't met the person before in this lifetime, but it could have been a former life.

The personal story of Florence and me, and all the stories in this book, are part of the mounting evidence to support the hypothesis of reincarnation. Of course, no one has yet proven reincarnation, but neither has anyone—scientist, theologian, or layman—satisfactorily refuted it.

The words *reincarnation, transmigration, palingenesis,* and *metempsychose* have the same intrinsic meaning, and some use them interchangeably. *Webster's New Twentieth Century Dictionary,* second edition, defines them as follows: Transmigration: "The supposed passing of the soul into another body after death; metempsychose." Metempsychose: "To translate from one body to another, as the soul." Palingenesis: "Birth over again; regeneration. That phase in the development of an individual plant or animal which repeats the evolutionary history of the group to which it belongs." Reincarnation: "Rebirth [of the soul] in another body." Reincarnation appears to be a normal continuity of what can be termed the Natural Law. Succinctly, according to Webster's dictionary,

"Natural Law [is] the laws of nature, collectively." If there is life after death, as is held, why shouldn't there be life before birth into this particular physical life? It satisfies an orderly, natural process we find throughout nature.

(Attempting to define this reincarnative postulate of Natural Law to mass satisfaction would be at once arbitrary and, certainly, endless. In our present context we are considering the principle of human physical birth, life, death, rebirth, ad infinitum, in kind. We don't want to emulate the centipede, who was once asked which of his many legs moved first and became so engrossed with this crashing phenomenon that he became catatonic and ceased functioning at all.)

The continuity of successive physical lives upon this (or another) planet by individual choice, as a particular experiencing lifetime, is conformable, naturalistic, progressive. To say that over a billion years our spaceship Earth developed as a water planet, then during another billion years life developed, and ultimately an amoeba hauled itself from the primordial ooze, and over eons of evolution became the entity known as man—that is more stupendous than to believe man has existed, been physically born and reborn through eternity, and peoples other planets in the vastness of the universe, or even that we were dropped off here on the planet Earth by more advanced galactic civilizations.

When the subject of reincarnation comes up in conversation, a frequent question is: "If I don't remember a past life, what's the point of having lived it?" Not only do the majority of us have no conscious memory of a past life but we can't remember most events from childhood. Those early years shaped our lives to a large extent, but they have faded from memory in just a few short earthly years as we changed, grew, and developed. Occasionally some present event will trigger the memory of an earlier similar happening. In obtaining my stories from people around the country, it was apparent in every case that those I talked to were convinced in their own minds that their problems in this life were the effect of some cause they had set in operation, either in this life or in a previous existence. We had long discussions about whether it is

The Return-Trip Ticket

merely chance that manifestly senseless tragedies strike some people; chance that fantastic success seems built into others for no apparent reason. If the conditions of life are merely hit-and-miss chance, then man is the only planetary subject/object to which this applies, an escape from the natural order.

The basis for this book, in our opinion, is that there *is* a reason for everything that does or does not happen to a person in this life. We in no way attempt to supply answers about reincarnation. The conjectures of each relator are very personal; although you might disagree with some of them, you will also be intrigued with the candidness they exhibit in their own beliefs. We did not use the stories obtained from those who saw themselves as having been the Virgin Mary, Jesus, Napoleon, Moses, John the Baptist, or Alexander the Great. My late friend, the trance medium Arthur Ford, told me he had personally met twenty-three people who believed they once were the Virgin Mary.

To preface this next, let me jot down a simplistic truth I'm old enough to have tested and found quite pure: If you believe, no explanation is necessary; if you don't believe, no explanation is possible.

I embrace the reincarnative principle as the only theory that makes any sense to me. I say this from my own concept that God is God and we are his kids. God is, was, and always has been, will always be. We are his kids and will be, likewise, eternal. I liken physical life to a hesitation waltz—we come into life momentarily, to learn something, perhaps pay for a former transgression or be rewarded for some accomplishment or deed in a former life. At one end of the monetary spectrum some come into millionaire families while others are born into grinding, lifelong poverty; some become the cream of upper-class society, but the majority of us don't reach that level, seem actually to be held back, compartmentalized.

The reincarnation hypothesis isn't as senseless as it might appear if we as individuals can be made to feel and accept that we are on an eternal voyage of mental, moral, emotional, and spiritual progression. It has been posited that we have, and no one knows when, fragmented from the godhead and are trying to find our way back. Each lifetime can be considered a period of that learning process as we unconsciously work with ourselves by divesting, honing, polishing, conquering, or abolishing whatever within us needs it. How long will it take? How long is it to eternity? Not long; we live in it.

Dr. Freda Morris points out in the introduction: "We have always repeated our lessons over and over in order to learn them thoroughly. Undoubtedly we must repeat our experiences as people over and over, too." It is comforting to think that we do have potential and will progress, slowly or rapidly, as we make our way back home.

A recent survey indicates that about 74 percent of the population of the United States believes in continuing life after death. The percentage believing in reincarnation is lower, but appreciably higher than it was just twenty-five years ago. If we have a soul, where does it go upon the death of the physical body? If it doesn't return here immediately, then perhaps to one of any number of other planets now believed to support life in our vast universe? In a jocular vein, it would seem that, if new life is breathed into each body, wherever the spirits of the deceased go they would have to have a tremendous amount of room, if they are indeed matter and have displacement. If spirit is matter, it possesses spatial properties and exists in space. Millions of operations upon the human body have never isolated or even detected the presence, let alone the location, of a spirit, although we acknowledge that the body is occupied by one. When the body dies, the spirit departs.

There is more evidence now for the existence of a viable spirit than there was in the days when Charles Darwin threw up his hands and declared, "I feel most deeply that this whole question of creation is too profound for human intellect. A dog might as well speculate on the mind of Newton! Let every man hope and believe what he can."

Lao Tzu (c. 604 B.C.) obviously didn't have Darwin's despair. He expressed it this way. "Birth is not a beginning; death not the end. There is existence with limitation; there is

The Return-Trip Ticket

continuity without a starting point. There is birth, there is death, there is issuing forth, there is entering in. That through which passes in and out without seeing its form, that is the Portal of Heavenly Tao."

He also said, "There is something which existed before Heaven and Earth. Oh how still it is, and formless, standing alone without changing, reaching everywhere without suffering harm. It must be regarded as the Mother of the Universe. It appears to be everlasting. Its name I know not. To designate it, I call it Tao."

Historically, over the centuries, there has been belief in reincarnation in Hinduism, Buddhism, Mohammedanism, Zoroastrianism, Judaism; in primitive and tribal religions (American Indians, Asians, Africans, Malayans, Australians); among the Greeks, Romans, British, French, Germans, Scandinavians, Russians; among great scientists, philosophers, naturalists, theosophists, writers, lecturers, astrologers, journalists, mystics, poets, historians, and theologians; and also in segments of contemporary Christianity. The notables who believed in reincarnation read like a who's who of history: Empedocles, Anaxagoras, Pythagoras, Plato, Aristotle, Apollonius, Plutarch, Plotinus. In Italy: Ovid, Cicero, Julius Caesar, Virgil, Sallust, Michelangelo, Tommaso Campanella. In Germany: Frederick the Great, Immanuel Kant, J. W. von Goethe, J. P. F. Richter, J. G. Fichte, G. W. F. Hegel, Friedrich von Schlegel, Karl Krause, Schopenhauer, Wagner, Heinrich Heine, Elizabeth of Austria, Nietzsche, Steiner, and Albert Schweitzer. In Judaism: Moses, King Solomon, Philo Judeus, Rabbi Chajim Vital, Rabbi Simeon ben Jochai, Rabbi Manasseh ben Israel, Sholem Asch. The list could be extended enormously.

In the third or fourth century A.D. some churchmen decreed that reincarnation was a whimsical myth, an unsupported fable to be shunned by the devout. The Pope said nothing at the time, giving rise to the legend that to Christians reincarnation was anathema. But somehow Roman Catholicism came to deny, and still denies, reincarnation. Some hold that it is an orthodox religious view that Christ did not believe in reincarnation, but Christ neither denied nor repudiated it. Reincarnation was (and is) a common Jewish belief. Interestingly, among other leading men of the Christian church, St. Augustine and St. Francis of Assisi accepted the idea of reincarnation.

In a discussion I had with a theologian, when I said my investigations revealed that over 600 million people on this planet believe in reincarnation, he became incensed and replied, "That doesn't make it true." Since he'd opened the door himself, I had to ask that if because hundreds of millions of Christians believe in the deity and resurrection of Christ it made it any more true. That constituted an impasse of gargantuan proportions. God hasn't been proved in the scientific laboratory.

I have also been asked, "Does a person reincarnate into another century or immediately?" It appears there is no set pattern. There are well-attested cases in the files involving a child of four or five who had such a vivid memory of an immediate past life that it was checked out and found true. In the foreword to Ian Stevenson's book on the subject, C. J. Ducasse comments, "Conceivably, however, survival, if it occurs, might take the form of reincarnation either immediately after death or perhaps after an interval of discarnate existence. This conception has not been widely entertained in the West, but its reasonableness has commended it to some of the most eminent thinkers who have given it attention." *

Memories of a former life are most likely among children; as the children grow older, their recollections fade as they are exposed to more orthodox societal and familial views. Where do these memories come from when they reach an adult? Through hypnosis and dreams (waking and sleeping) many people have relived scenes that have not occurred in this life, and have even dreamed of being someone else. These dreams are presumed to come from one of a number of sources: from the individual's own former life, through a race memory, or through the agency of a discarnate entity beaming its own

* See Ian Stevenson, "Twenty Cases Suggestive of Reincarnation" (New York: American Society for Psychical Research, 1966).

memory to the remembering individual. If that last could be considered picking up the memory from cosmic consciousness, the question must be: How can it be so specific as to remember addresses or names of close relatives?

As physically incarnate beings, we have problems and will continue to be beset with problems. And we are all seeking answers to them. Any one of us—titled, degreed, frocked, unfrocked, overalled, long-haired, or undressed—is entitled to as much conjecture as the next. People who don't have pretty heavy living problems usually don't visit astrologers, clairvoyants, or mediums. I did because science and theology weren't providing sufficient answers. Astrology, presently called an occult science, supplied a particularly substantial foothold. It gave me reasons why certain things were happening to, with, and around me. These reasons proved valid and took me through a pretty rough, long period in my life. As was explained, I was "paying my Karma."

In two years of traveling across the United States in search of reincarnation stories I have yet to come up with anyone who has a solid memory of having been a cow in former life —or a horse, a dog, a cat, a rock, or a tree. But, some have questioned, isn't it possible that an architect in this life could have been a beaver in a former life; an Olympic runner, a cheetah; a weight lifter, a gorilla or a bull? Stretch that as far as you like and you may have trouble keeping a straight face in front of some of your friends.

My own spiritual, emotional, and intellectual wonder and belief continue to expand as I seek answers, while I contemplate the vast concept of God exhibited in everything in the universe. Not one single thing has been left to chance. Man tries to interpret, but only God is the expert.

2

Types of Recall

During sleep it isn't unusual for people to see (or experience) themselves in a different time and place. They may be clothed in the manner of those they see around them, perhaps they are on another planet and converse in a strange tongue, but they know what they are saying and understand what others are saying to them, even though they may not in this life know any language but English. It has been posited that if an individual is watching himself doing something in a dream, standing off to one side, the experience is truly a dream and not the recognition of an actual past or present occurrence. If he is physically doing the action taking place, possibly the experience is Dreaming True, "You Are There." Also, when the dreamer is an observer watching something happen, he can be experiencing precognition, seeing an event that is going to happen in the near or distant future. Then there is clairvoyance, mentally picking up something that is taking place at the time it is dreamed of, or suddenly seeing it in a waking state.

Usually children have no idea of the reincarnation concept,

but many of them do have various astounding abilities that, for lack of any other explanation, could have come over with them from a former life. A four-year-old girl played the piano before she could talk; a boy began learning Hebrew at age three and at age seven was declared by experts to have exhibited a better knowledge of Hebrew than many candidates three times his age who were seeking fellowships with leading universities, and at thirteen the boy had mastered thirteen other languages. Then there is Plato's "Theory of Reminiscence": "Knowledge easily acquired is that which the enduring self had in an earlier life, so that it flows back easily." Memory brought over? It appears so.

Clairvoyance (clear seeing) is another suggestion in the reincarnation proposal. Jack George, age twelve, was driving with his folks from Missouri to California. About ten miles from a remote old town in Arizona, a place he had never heard of, in a state he had never been in, he suddenly began describing the town, giving the names and descriptions of various business buildings on the main street. When the family arrived, the street and buildings were exactly as young Jack had said they were. Yes, what occurred could have been clairvoyance—I failed to mention that during his account of the place he excitedly said "that is how they were when I was there."

Searing skepticism used to suppress the reincarnation theory leads one to ruminate on the old saw, "The lady doth protest too much, methinks."

You walk into a room, or down the street of a strange town, and suddenly you experience what is known as déjà vu (French for "already seen"; in psychology, the illusion that one has previously had a given experience). The room or the street, the houses, the wash on the line in a backyard, all are completely familiar although you've never been there before in this life. Déjà vu is quite common and vast numbers of us have experienced it; it is an eerie, weird feeling. After we reach adulthood, it doesn't seem to occur as frequently, although people in their sixties and seventies report they experience it once in a while.

Have you really been there? There are three theories postulated for this phenomenon.

1. You have been there in a former life.

2. The eye (conscious mind), seeing, transmits the observed image to the subconscious; on the way to the subconscious there is a lightninglike break in the electrical transmission—the image is immediately shortcircuited, instantly thrown back in an unanswered form—and because of faulty transmission you have the definite feeling you've been there.

3. An entity on the other side, close to you at the moment, was there during its physical life and transmits the memory to you; you pick it up and receive a definite impression of having been there, or having witnessed the same scene previously.

Receiving impressions from physically living persons, or from people who have just died, or from those already on the other side for some time provides the case for survival of physical death. There are numerous medical articles on what are called deathbed observations, and I refer specifically to "Deathbed Observations by Physicians and Nurses," by Karlis Osis.*

> In the minds of many people hallucinations are associated with something morbid and insane. This is, however, an outdated concept, for imagery is in fact a normal part of our lives. When images emerge involuntarily and are accompanied by a complete or partial sense of reality, we call them hallucinations. Normal people experience them, and they are common among artists and inventors. We might even call them an integral part of creative activity. The same kinds of experience often occur during sleep and then we simply call them dreams.

Further on in this monograph:

> Of the patterns we found, all are necessarily exploratory, except for two: (1) the fact that most phantasms (hallucinatory figures) are of the dead and (2) that they are apparitional in nature (the surroundings are perceived as

normal). These two trends were clearly emphasized by Hyslop and by Barrett who presented the so-called "Peak in Darien" hypothesis prominent in discussion for half a century. A "Peak in Darien" example is quoted by Hart from Barrett's *Deathbed Visions:* "On January 12, 1924, a Mrs. B. was dying in a hospital in England. Her sister Vida had died on December 25, 1923, but her illness and death had been carefully kept from Mrs. B. because of her own serious illness. As Mrs. B. was sinking, she said: 'It is all so dark, I cannot see.' A moment later her face brightened, and she exclaimed: 'Oh, it is lovely and bright; you cannot see as I can.' A little later she said: 'I can see father; he wants me, he is so lonely.' Then, with a rather puzzled expression: 'He has Vida with him,' turning to her mother— 'Vida is with him!' A few moments later she died."

William James (*Varieties of Religious Experience*), felt that hallucinations were of distinctive importance and might be genuine. G. N. M. Tyrell, in *Apparitions,* found substantial evidence in that some hallucinations connect completely subjective forms with a cognizance of external reality, accomplished by extrasensory information.

Let's take a look at a moment-of-death occurrence with which I am personally familiar. It took place between my mother and me during a dream I had, and approximately at the moment she expired. This is not unusual in the annals of the phenomenon of continuing life.

She's on Her Way

In November 1967 my wife constructed an astrological chart on me and was in the process of reading it. She'd been working with it for a couple of days and would take a break every so often for a cup of coffee and a stretch. One evening I was sitting in the front room learning my lines for an upcoming role in a "Daniel Boone" television show.

---

* Karlis Osis, "Deathbed Observations by Physicians and Nurses," *Parapsychology Monograph,* no. 3 (New York: Parapsychology Foundation, 1961).

Florence came into the room, seated herself on the couch across from me, and, when she thought I'd come to a stopping place, she interrupted. It was evident she was disturbed. Possessed of a keen mind and a powerful personality, her presence doesn't pass unnoticed. If she's in a happy mood, the room lights up; if she's down, she carries it like a black torch that permeates every nook and cranny.

"I don't like something I see in your chart. I've checked and rechecked it," she said.

I automatically tuned myself for bad aspects, braced, and waited.

"It concerns a woman in your life; I see a powerful separative aspect coming up. I can't tell which woman—me or your mother."

Sensing immediately that she actually was equating that aspect with herself, I tried to take the onus off by suggesting that perhaps it meant any one of four women in my life—wife, mother, or two daughters back east.

"No, this woman is close to you, living with you. It shows that on or about February 2, 1968, there is a fatal aspect for a woman in your life."

I continued to try to get her off dead center. "All right, why get uptight and freak now? February is three and a half months away; and anyway, that nonsense can flip you out. Stop reading it."

It is easy for an astrologer to go back to a chart and find reasons why such-and-such happened; the difficult, and often dangerous, thing is to read ahead. The trends are present in a chart, and in the hands of a topflight astrologer they can be interpreted, sometimes with uncanny accuracy.

My mother had been in ailing health for many years, having spent thirty-five years of her life either on crutches or in a wheelchair. I'd forgotten the omen when, in the latter part of January 1968, my mother developed a chest congestion and we had the doctor in, just to be on the safe side. He diagnosed it as a light case of upper respiratory pneumonia, gave her shots, and prescribed the necessary medication. The following day he visited her and became alarmed because her condi-

The Return-Trip Ticket

tion had worsened, but he still allowed her to remain home.

I had to fly to Odessa, Texas, that same day. When I returned home the night of February 1, Florence told me my mother had been taken to the hospital. I called the hospital and was told she was resting comfortably and I could see her in the morning. The following morning, February 2, the hospital called and informed me that my mother had had a stroke and was in a coma. There could be no visitors; the hospital staff was doing what it could for her. I talked on the phone with the doctor and the head nurse, and they assured me everything medically possible was being done. My mother's condition remained stable for the next two days; she didn't rally at any time. I visited the hospital each day and stood by at home in case I was called.

During sleep, on the morning of February 5, I had a dream in which my mother was present as a young girl, well and strong. I didn't see myself in the dream but was an observer. We were in a field and she was running and skipping gaily about. Finally she came toward me, laughing. As she reached out to touch me, the dream ended abruptly. I awoke as though someone had physically touched or shaken me. Florence was sleeping soundly and there wasn't anyone else in the room. I got up and wandered through the house, checking the front, side, and back doors, which were locked. When I crawled back into bed, I noted that the time was a few minutes after three o'clock. At nine o'clock that morning the hospital called to inform me that my mother had passed on at seven-thirty, an hour and a half prior to the call.

I went to the hospital. After collecting my mother's belongings, I stood in the corridor outside her room talking with the head nurse. We were alone when I came out with it and said, "She passed away at three o'clock this morning, didn't she?"

She was startled, glanced quickly about us, and then said in a low voice, "Why do you say that?"

I told her of my dream, of my mother reaching out to touch me, of the dream ending with my feeling that someone had actually touched me, awakening me. I told her I thought the staff had given my mother's time of death as seven-thirty because that was when the doctor arrived to verify it and sign the certificate.

Again, she glanced about us, then said, "Don't say anything to anyone—it wouldn't serve any purpose—but I was on duty at three o'clock and that is the time she went." She went on to tell me that nurses often hear of this sort of thing happening. She, too, was convinced that departing spirits have their own way of communicating with loved ones or close friends as they are released from physical life and enter the next plane. "She wanted to let you know that she was on her way," the nurse said.

I believe my mother was communicating with me telepathically, through the hallucination of my dream, I personally, have had no further contact with her, either physical or pyschic, dream or other hallucination.

This next account might be termed a waking hallucination —keeping in mind that a definition of hallucination is "The apparent perception of sights and sounds, etc., that are not actually present." Or are those sights and sounds actually present and perceivable for some people? The man who told the story to me said he had not read any material about the place he was visiting at the time this phenomenon transpired. He can't interpret the incident except as a possible on-the-spot reincarnative recollection.

You Were Here, Too

The popular character actor Robert Middleton and I were appearing in a movie being made in Dallas, Texas, entitled *Help Stamp Out Fair Play*. Bob lives only a few minutes from me in California's San Fernando Valley, but we had to go to Texas to meet!

In looking for material for this book, I have found that when I bring up the subject of reincarnation one of two things happens—either I get a lot of static, and get soundly trounced verbally in some cases, or I do get a story. My approach has become pretty direct; I may ask, "Do you think you have lived a former life, reincarnated?" I put it that bluntly to Bob. He looked at me for a moment to see if I was putting him on. Then, in his deep Taurian voice, he said, "Reincarnation? Hmmm. I have a story you might be interested in. I think it's reincarnation." He wouldn't go into it on the set, so we agreed to have dinner that night so I could record his tale.

A few years ago Bob, along with a couple of other noted people, was the guest of the Turkish minister of tourism. They were originally going to the city of Antalya to see the Turkish Riviera; but at the last moment the plans were changed and the minister suggested a visit to the ancient city of Izmir, on the west coast of Turkey. About two hundred miles north is the city of Troy, and another site of great historical significance is the ruins of the city of Ephesus. According to Bob's guide, who was on the faculty of one of the Turkish universities, there were four successive cities of Ephesus, all in the same area, each of which was destroyed by an earthquake, a war, or a disaster of one sort or another.

As the group approached the ruins, the entire city appeared to be excavated from a very narrow valley with steep sides like a huge ravine. It had been covered over by centuries of drifting dust and debris, which had completely blanketed it to quite a depth. The workmen had excavated the central section of the city on both sides of the valley. They had not gone back into excavating the surrounding hills yet, but there was evidence that there were buildings there that correspond to our apartment buildings of today, though on a much smaller scale.

It was Bob's first exposure to an ancient site, and it proved exciting from more than just an archeological standpoint. It was during the month of January and the visitors were practically alone with the guide; they were not jostled by hordes of tourists or blistered by the ferocious heat of the later season. As they walked down what is called the Marble Street, the guide bent over, picked up a small shard of marble about an inch in diameter, and extended it to Bob, saying, "Here. You never know—Cleopatra may have walked on this piece of marble. She and Antony walked up the street after they landed here, and they came up this way."

Bob found himself emotionally being drawn back through the centuries. As the visitors were preparing to leave Ephesus, the guide said there was one place he wanted them to see— the shrine where John brought the Virgin Mary after the crucifixion of Christ, which also was the place where Mary had lived out her life. The ruins had become a shrine after they had been restored. The guide drove the visitors to the site, a few miles from Ephesus. The only person present when they arrived was a French abbé whose sole function was to look after the shrine and continue the restoration work. It was a little stone building no more than about twenty to twenty-five feet square. The visitors were shown pictures of what the abode had looked like prior to its restoration, and they were ushered inside.

Straight in, at the front entrance, against the back wall, was the shrine. To the right was another shrine, a Mohammedan one that faced Mecca. Bob took a look at the Mohammedan shrine, then went over to see the Christian one. By this time, the others had left the room and he was alone. While he was standing at the shrine, he heard what could have been a sound but wasn't. It wasn't a wail, nor a voice, yet it had a human quality, as though someone was trying to speak. It was low and slow, a disrhythmic rise and fall of cadence. At first he thought it was the wind blowing through the small cracks in the building.

While he was standing in the middle of the room, something seemed to draw him toward the back wall. He hadn't been cold when he came in, but now he developed a chill, a cold, prickly feeling. The others called to him from outside. He answered that he would be right with them, but he couldn't move.

"I was held there. I couldn't turn away. As I stood there, I became aware of a figure moving about in the room. As it passed me, on my left, it turned and looked directly at me— it was almost a physical impact. It was the face and clothed figure of what I can only describe as an ancient monk. The face was unlined, but somber. The eyes were deepset; there was an intensity leaping from them that was unmistakably alive. My whole physical being just seemed to dissolve insofar as my feeling of being me in the present was concerned. I became the monk, physically, actually, right there in the shrine. How else can I explain it but that I stepped out of me and into the monk? Immediately I knew who I was, and I could see the Bob Middleton—*me*—standing there.

"I also, as the monk, knew I had been present at the time the Virgin Mary had been either in that building or in that area. Obviously, then, I had been a contemporary of her son, Jesus, but I have no recollection of it. As the monk, I don't feel I really belonged in the building but was rather a visitor. It was the most natural thing in the world for me to go over to the shrine and kneel for a moment. Then I got up, turned toward the door, and as I passed my own Robert Middleton body I became myself again, stepped back into myself. The monk was gone, and the low-voice cadence was also gone. I stood there for another minute or two, but nothing more happened."

Very reluctantly, Bob turned and left the building, hanging back, walking slowly after the others. The French abbé came over to him when he stopped to look back, and said, "I can tell that you know, too."

Bob looked at him for a moment and said, "I know what?"

The monk replied, "You were here, too."

Bob then told the monk what had happened and was informed that this happened to others infrequently. It is now thought, the abbé added, that those who have this experience were at one time physically present in the shrine and relive a few moments of it. Bob had been caught up in what might be called a replay of the memory tape of time. But how did he step out of his body and into that of the monk? Did he step out of his body, have an out-of-body experience, and then step back into the body of that monk? Was he reliving a moment of life when he was that monk, some two thousand years before? There hadn't been any whirlwind rush of sequences in his being drawn back; rather it was like the slow dissolves from one successive scene after another—the main scene was played out, the scenes dissolved forward, and the present physical scene continued.

It was all very familiar to him, in the same way that the present life is familiar to the person living it. Bob is Jewish and has no feeling for Christian shrines other than that of an impartial interest. He explained to me, "I only wish I were more experienced in receiving psychic impressions. Perhaps I could relive much more, know more about who I was and what I was doing in that area at that distant time. As I tell you of the experience now, I get the same chill, as though somebody is reaching out to me, trying to crystallize a memory, either vocally or physically. I was that monk, and that monk was me."

The abbé told Bob that when John brought Mary there the building was already in existence—where the fireplace was then the shrine is today. When he saw himself in the building, it was as if he completely knew his way around, had been there many times before, and knew why he was there. As the monk, when he looked at the backdrop of the room, at the smoke stains on the wall, and around the fireplace and on the ceiling, he was looking at very familiar things.

Bob went to Israel the following week, wandered around in the old sections of the towns, and received some of the same feelings, but they were not as strong as they had been in the shrine near Ephesus. He didn't "see" himself. To him, as a Jew, it would have been more significant to have had those feelings and impressions when he visited the burial place of King David on Mt. Sinai. But no, it was in the Christian shrine that he literally "saw" himself, was himself, in another life.

On one other occasion Bob experienced a similar recall of some other lifetime: "When I was a young boy, I remember being taken to a horse farm in Kentucky that had been built about 1810. The moment we entered the gates of the farm, I knew I had been there before. The people I was with were amazed at how I knew my way around the place, where things were. I don't know how it happened, but I'd been there before, too. Perhaps as a member of the family, maybe as a worker? I knew the whole place like my own house and backyard."

I Was a Courtesan—and a Murderer

Hazel is the wife of Hollywood director and actor Bob Bauder. Bob dropped by one day while I was typing up another of the stories and wanted to know what I was doing. When I told him, he said, "Hey, you oughta talk to Hazel, she's got a couple of weirdos." And I did. She was delighted, when I didn't think her stories were "weirdos."

Hazel is in her middle thirties, of medium height and dark-haired. She has large, expressive brown eyes and is physically well endowed by nature. I've known the Bauders for a few years and she has never appeared to be the nervous type. Bob has been congratulated on having a mate who wouldn't panic, get overly upset, or be downright depressed by the vicissitudes that beset most show business people from time to time, such as being out of work for long periods.

To my knowledge, Hazel has not overtly exhibited flights of wild fancy and action, such as practicing yoga in the nude or "streaking" across crowded thoroughfares. Outwardly, she is a normal, well-balanced girl of good intellect to whom many pour out their troubles, and from whom they seek advice. At the time I obtained her story, Hazel had stepped into the breach of one of Bob's "dry" periods and was a department manager in a nationally known women's apparel chain store in the San Fernando Valley.

Hazel recalls things during the night when she's dreaming. Or is she dreaming? She's not sure. If it had happened once or twice, not much would be thought about it, but it has happened a couple of times a month for at least the last two years. It's always the same dream, but each time there is some new little something added, making the picture a bit larger. The scene she describes is in Paris. She has never been to France in this lifetime, so she has never had the opportunity to confirm the existence of the places she recalls. In the dreams she is never the observer; she is the person doing the action.

"It is late afternoon and I'm stepping out of a carriage. The door of the carriage has a crest on it, and I'm being helped by a footman dressed in livery. Both the coachman and the footman are in silk trousers and white stockings and brocaded hats. As the footman helps me out of the coach, I see that I have jeweled slippers on my feet and my costume is heavy blue satin, with a low décolleté neckline. I'm wearing lots of diamonds and a hooded heavy blue velvet coat trimmed in ermine, and my hands are shoved into a big ermine muff. I have a maid with me, and she alights from the carriage after me. We speak French. I've never learned French in this lifetime, but I'm good at it when I'm back there.

"I'm ushered through a gate that is opened by guards, and they bow and scrape to me. One of the guards accompanies us down a corridor that seems to be dark and damp, like a back entrance. As we go along the corridor, I hang back and take a left turn into another corridor. I'd been here before, and had been denied going this way on other visits, so when I see my chance I turn off to see what was denied me.

"I come to a heavy door that is difficult to open. When I step inside the room, I see cages full of people. Men, women, children even, all ages, cooped up like animals, dressed in rags, and the stench of unwashed bodies is terrific. They begin grabbing at me through the bars, screaming some name at me that I can't remember, or it just doesn't register. They are saying that I am a part of all their misery, me and all my finery and high living. I keep back from the cages, and can hear myself trying to tell them it isn't my fault, and I whimper and cry because I'm so scared.

"The maid and the guard come running in and are very upset. The guard says, 'You shouldn't be in here, this is the wrong place for you. Please don't tell anyone you were here.'

"They take me out, back down the corridor, and we go through a heavy metal door and through a gate that has to be opened by another guard dressed much more resplendently then the one I am with. We go along a cobblestone hallway and come to a beautiful wooden door that is all hand-carved. Beyond that is a massive marble hallway that is carpeted in one long, deep-piled rug with big jeweled mirrors on gold walls. At another huge carved door we stop while the guard knocks.

"When the door is opened, I enter by myself. It is a huge room, beautifully appointed, and done in a lot of gold leaf. The rug again is red. Down at the end of the room there appears to be a huge chair or a throne. There is a man sitting in it. I walk the entire length of the room, and as I pass a mirror I see myself. I'm wearing jewels and my hair is coiffed in a heavy white pompadour. As I come to the chair, the man rises to greet me. I've never really been able to distinguish what he looks like, but he is very pleasant to me. He takes me by the arm and says that we are going out to dine at my favorite place."

In an extension of this dream Hazel finds herself in a restaurant or dining place. She isn't sure whether it is within the palace or somewhere outside. There are other people there, but she doesn't know who they are. The room is done in heavy reds and brightly polished dark wood. The tableware is gold and silver, with beautiful crystal glasses and gold leaf plates. The waiters come and bow and scrape to her and the man.

"I have no recollection of when I might have changed clothes, but now I'm wearing all sable—a full-length sable coat with hood. A darling little boy comes over to my table and talks to me. He has dark brown curly hair and he's wearing a cossack hat, boots, and loose blouse and trousers. He speaks to me in French and I answer him. He kisses my hand, and then a woman comes over to us and tells me that she is his mother, and they leave."

Hazel's next recollection seems to be later that night. She and the man are out on the street.

"It must have been in the fall or winter because the leaves have fallen from the trees and it is snowing. I hear a noise and look down the street. A wagon full of men comes into sight; they are fighting among themselves, yelling and shouting and throwing wine bottles. They throw things at us and we duck."

Hazel did not at any time step outside of herself and become an observer. She is certain that she was that woman, that she was there in person.

"If the dream only happened once or twice I wouldn't think much about it—it would just be interesting—but it's too frequent. I always look forward to dreaming the whole sequence and hope something new will be added—that maybe I will find out who I really am, or was."

At no time during the dreams does she have the feeling of going out of her body, of doing astral projection. The experience, to her, is as real as everyday living, but the features of the people she's with are blurred and indistinct. She does not feel that she was a queen at that time, or a lady of high rank. On the contrary, because she was ushered into the palace through what seemed to be a dungeon corridor, she believes the meeting was something clandestine.

"If anything, instead of being a queen or a great lady, I think I might have been a courtesan. If there is ever an end to the story, it will probably be when I'm banished, or imprisoned, or guillotined!"

And this is not the only "dream" that Hazel has had of a former existence. Most people I've interviewed don't recall more than one past life, but Hazel also told me of one she wasn't exactly proud of. In this other recollection she was a boy, and it could have been in the same period—the seventeenth or eighteenth century. She was about twenty years old, and she was not dressed very well but in shoddy, dirty clothes.

"I'm walking down this street and it's night. I look around and then climb a high wall. There is a huge house behind the wall. I prowl around until I find something to climb up and then I go into a room. I can see there are two people sleeping in a big bed. I tiptoe around the room looking everything over, looking for something to steal. I find a big box on a dresser and open it. There are some heavy bright objects in it, like bracelets and pendants. I scoop up a lot of things and stuff them in my pockets.

"Then there is a noise from the bed and I look over to see one of the people reach out and pull at a long cord hanging from the ceiling alongside the bed. Both of the people sit up. I quickly pull a knife out of my waistband and run over and stab them. I kill them both, the man first. I go back out the way I came in, over the wall and disappear down the street. If that is a past life, then I was a boy, I was a thief, and I was a murderer. That's all I can remember."

The fragmentation of people's recollections is frustrating. How gratifying it would be if those who have reincarnative recollections could begin at the very beginning, outline the whole sequence in detail, and know the ending. But that would be asking too much, I know. Infrequently someone will come up with details you feel might be checked out to the complete satisfaction of researchers, but usually it just doesn't happen that way.

I Only Draw Black People

A friend in Los Angeles told me about a white woman in Dallas, Texas, who is an artist but only draws pictures and portraits of black people. She had told him something about this being a reincarnative carryover from a former life when she was black. At about the same time I had an offer from a movie producer in Dallas, inviting me to come down and do a role in a picture he was making. It was a great opportunity: a salary, transportation, room and board, and (I hoped) another story.

When I arrived in Dallas, I checked into my suite at the hotel and called the producer to tell him I was on board. Then I looked in the phone book, got Donna's number, and called her. I was in luck. Yes, she was Donna ―――――. After introducing myself and telling her why I was in Dallas, I went right into my reason for calling her and said I was doing a manuscript on people who feel they have had reincarnative recollections or experiences.

There was nothing guarded about her reply; she merely said the story was too long to be done over the phone. We set up an appointment for dinner at my hotel. For purposes of identification in the lobby I asked her if she had ever watched "Captain Midnight" on television. I could see her smile as she replied, "Yes. I'll recognize you before you do me."

This story had really excited me when the fellow told me about it in Los Angeles, so I did some speculating while I was prowling around the lobby waiting for Donna. What would she look like? How would she dress? Was she some kind of nut or was she putting people on for purposes of capitalizing? I couldn't tell much from our short telephone conversation. It had been just that—conversational. Her voice was well modulated, her manner pleasant; she sounded educated.

Donna is a comely, fair girl in her thirties with chestnut brown hair and green eyes flecked with brown. She is a slender five feet six inches tall. She was wearing a beige and white striped knee-length dress with long sleeves and carrying a brown artist's portfolio. Those were my initial impressions when a woman's voice turned me around by saying, "I never thought I would meet Captain Midnight in person."

We will now do some quick cuts and dissolves by saying that we spent more than three hours getting the facts of her two lives, discussing reincarnation. Here is what the finished picture looked like.

Donna was about eleven or twelve years old in this life when she began to have memories of her former life. The memories were like waking dream sequences. It wasn't a constant thing, but when she had one of the "dreams" it was of a certain, specific time and included everything that happened at that time. Donna's urge to draw had begun when she was a little girl in New York City, in grammar school. She had a natural talent for drawing, and continued her work into high school and during her three years at City College in New York.

Her paintings were always, unless she was told to do otherwise, of black people.

"I was a boy. There are no records, but I'm pretty sure my name was Grant. I lived on a plantation right near Lake Pontchartrain, about fifteen miles from it, and about sixty miles from New Orleans. The time I lived there was approximately between 1835 and 1864. It could have been before 1835 that I was born, but I always see myself as around twenty-nine or thirty years old when a lot of us got smallpox and I died of it.

"I don't remember my father in that lifetime at all. There were just three of us—my mother, my brother, and me. My mother was in charge of getting the laundry out for the whole place—for the whites, that is, because the slaves all did their own washing and cleaning. Mother usually worked mostly up at the main house, overseeing the linen supply, and she would take me along to help her. As I say, I was about eleven or twelve years old at the time.

"The old master had a wife and some children, one of whom was a girl. I don't remember them too well, but the girl had a drawing board or easel and I used to watch her for hours on end. It fascinated me to see the painting take shape —how she would do the background and then put in the figures. I would go out to the trash heap and get pieces of paper and cardboard that had been thrown away and use mud as my paint, and I got pretty good at it.

"One day I had been helping my mother in the big house and I wandered into the room where Little Missy did her painting. There was no one around, so I began drawing a picture in paint, of a man. I guess I had the thing pretty well along when I was caught. The old master came charging into the room and grabbed me, and spanked me something good. All the slaves learned early in life to make a big fuss when they were spanked or whipped for something, and I did my best to convince him he was practically killing me. The cries brought all the slaves in the house, and the master's wife and kids. The old master wasn't angry because I used the paints; what he absolutely forbid me to ever do was draw a picture of a white person. Don't get the idea the old master was mean to us; from what I found out later, when I was older, he treated us as well as, if not better than, other slave-owners, but he wanted to make an impression on me. He did.

"While I was sniffling over in the corner, after the whipping, I heard them talking about the drawing. The old master couldn't believe it had been done by an illiterate Negro slave boy. Under the pain of another whipping he asked me if I'd done the drawing and I told him yes. After that Little Missy would give me sheets of drawing paper and even let me use her leftover paints. I guess the work was pretty good, because our owner would keep them in the big house and when company came he would display them and even send for me so the white visitors could look at me. All my pictures, of course, were of black people.

"When I was about eighteen, the old master took me to New Orleans with him, and I got the biggest jolt of my life when we went to the slave market and I watched the blacks being sold, auctioned like horses or cattle. Anyhow, the old master had taken some of my paintings with him. He put them up for sale, and people bought some of them. He even gave me some money; I don't remember how much, but I felt like a king when I was able to buy myself a pair of Spanish sandals—my very own shoes bought with my own money.

"When I was about twenty-five, I remember there was a big stir because some man from the museum in New York was coming to see the old master about my paintings. They even gave me some new clothes so I would be presentable, had me all shined up. The man from the North must have liked the pictures because he gave the old master what looked to me like all the money in the whole world, and took most of my paintings with him when he left. Since I was his slave, the old master put his own last name on the portraits.

"By this time I was employed mostly in the house—running errands, helping out in the kitchen with the housework, a general handyboy. I still couldn't read or write, but they let me have paints and drawing paper whenever I wanted it. The only thing they wouldn't let me do was 'draw on the job.' It had to be at night, or anytime I had off, and I remember they gave my mother a big, brighter-than-usual coal-oil lamp for me to use at night to work by.

"People from the other plantations and from New Orleans would come to see my paintings, and they bought some of them. The old master allowed me to sleep in the big house. My parlor and bedroom was a cubbyhole right under the circular staircase in the main hall, but it was like a palace to me. And I was allowed one day a week when I could stay in the 'painting room' and do nothing but draw my pictures. That was about as close to heaven as I got in that lifetime. As I said, the smallpox came and I got sick, and that's all I remember. I don't remember dying, but all memory or recollections stop then, so I must have died."

After Donna left school, and before she moved to Dallas, she worked as a commercial artist for advertising agencies in Manhattan, but the memories of her former life became so strong that she decided she had to visit the places she just knew she remembered. After she'd saved enough money, she and a venturesome girl friend took a vacation and went to New Orleans with the avowed intent of investigating the area. The girls drove out the highway from New Orleans, north on Route 51, skirting Lake Pontchartrain. They wound up in a small town alongside the highway, where Donna found the plantation she was looking for. She met the present owners of the now rundown estate. On the pretext of wanting to do a painting of the place, she was able to get a tour. The old slave quarters were gone, but she found the location of the old cabin where she had been born and raised. In the house she found one of the paintings "Grant" had done, although the present occupants said it was done by their great-grandfather. What's more, she bought the painting.

"Yes, I have the painting. It's in New York. It's of a Negro boy, a boy with full Negro features. The Basuto Negro is probably the purest of strains in the country, and I don't remember how I came to draw the subject, but the old master was always bringing someone new around for me to paint. Maybe it was me, although it doesn't look like me in my dream sequences. When I first saw the painting, I didn't get that bell-ringing in the solar plexus like you do when something strikes you as being right. It was just a picture, but I knew I had done it, back then.

"When I was a young girl, my folks used to ask me why I always drew pictures of black people. I couldn't tell them, just that I liked to draw pictures of Negroes more than I did white people. I'm thirty-four now, four or five years over the age when I died as the slave boy, Grant. I have no interest now in painting pictures of white people. As you can see, my drawings are all of black subjects."

The twelve-by-six portrait book she handed me was about three inches thick, and all the photographed paintings were of black people—men, women, children, babies, farm scenes, street scenes, you name it. There were no whites present in any of them.

"Donna, you say you went back to the old plantation. What kind of feelings did you have when you recognized the place—knew that this was the place you'd been a slave?"

"Oh, if you mean was I angry, or had a bitter feeling—no, it was more like I was visiting home. I wanted to cry, not because I'd been a slave, just because it was so familiar. I didn't have any particular feelings toward the present owners. I felt sorry for them. The place is practically a wreck, and they try to keep up appearances. It was always clean and neat when I lived there, or we—my people and I—lived there. No, I wasn't bitter. Anyway, the present owners haven't been involved with slaves—that was before their time."

"You say you were a young man about twenty-nine or thirty? What about being married? Do you remember being married?"

"Not married, but I have memories of a girl of my own race. The master didn't care whether we blacks married or not, but all the plantation owners wanted their slaves to have children—that way they didn't have to buy them, just see that they got born and raised. I don't remember whether the girl and I had any children, but chances are we did. Seems funny —if I had children in those days they would have called me Daddy—if my descendants are still alive today, and they probably are, they would have to call me grandmother!"

3

We've Known Each Other in Many Lifetimes

The first time Florence and I saw each other was in a restaurant called the Hofbrau in Astoria, Long Island. I'd never been in the place before, was accompanying a young lady I had just recently met. We were sitting at a table getting soused on Coca Cola, watching the other young people dance to a jukebox. Suddenly my eyes traveled toward the door, where three or four young people were entering. I locked in on the dark-haired girl with the three boys. She locked in on me. It was as though everything stopped.

I had the strongest urge to get up, go to her, and say, "How've you been?" In those days you didn't do that; you waited or wangled an introduction. The girl finally moved on, but during the next hour or two we practically never took our eyes off one another. None of that coy boy-sees-girl, girl-sees-boy, and they play bat-the-eyesies. This was an immediate psychic recognition.

Neither of us approached the other. When my date decided it was time to leave, I maneuvered to pass the table where she sat, paused for a moment, and placed a twenty-five-year commemorative school button I'd been wearing beside her Coke with the words, "Here's something to remember me by."

The following week I was invited to a party at a home on Long Island. Not long after I'd arrived, who should walk in but the fascinating girl with whom I had such an indefinable rapport. Again she was with someone else, but she detached the moment we saw each other, marched right up to me, and with Gemini straightforwardness she said, "Do you remember me?" We spent the rest of the evening deep in conversation. On parting I obtained her promise to see me the following night.

That was the beginning, in this life at least. We went together for over a year. I was in no position to ask a girl to marry me. I had decided to become an actor. Deciding is one thing, accomplishing it is something else!

But meanwhile I got a job in the tool room of the Anchor Cap and Closure Company, at which I lasted two months. Then I got some photographic modeling jobs, posing evenings for sculpting classes. At the end of the next six months I sold a pint of blood to pay my mounting bills. The intense feelings between Florence and me hadn't abated one bit, but her own innate protective instinct, plus the blandishments of her well-meaning parents, suggested nothing but complete disaster in a marital situation.

In desperation I joined the army. At first I was stationed at Governor's Island, in New York, near enough that I could see Florence once a month, but I was transferred to the Panama Canal Zone. We corresponded during my two years in Panama, until Florence wrote of her engagement and pending marriage to someone else.

When my tour of duty was over, I elected to be discharged from the service in California, with the idea of getting to Hollywood and becoming a movie actor.

I wrote Florence once in a while, telling her how the career was staggering along or zooming ahead, as the case might be, and didn't mind when I received no reply.

One day in August 1941 I felt absolutely compelled to go

for a swim at Santa Monica Beach, a place I'd never been; I really didn't know why I was going. While I was lying there on the sand, a dark-haired young lady walked over and said, "Hello. Remember me?" It was Florence. She and her husband were in California on a vacation; this was their last day and, as Florence explained later, she had adamantly insisted that they spend it at Santa Monica Beach, a place she'd never been either. We talked for a few minutes, and then we parted again.

After World War II began, I went back into the army, and during the war I was married. Following the war, I returned to Hollywood with my family and resumed my contract with Paramount Studio. My marriage had been creaking along for some time and finally broke down completely.

At that time Hollywood had the idea of sending Bundles to Britain by way of a Friendship Train. A whole flock of flatcars and boxcars were loaded with food and clothing. The train had been placed on the streetcar tracks on Hollywood Boulevard. It was to roll across Los Angeles, switch to the rail line, and proceed across country picking up stuff for ultimate shipment overseas. Each major studio had loaded a separate flatcar with actors and actresses to kick off the trek. I was on the Paramount car, along with such stars as Ray Milland, Bill Holden, Alan Ladd, and William Bendix. As I sat looking out over all the faces, I saw a very familiar one smiling up at me. It was Florence. She had been divorced for over a year and had come to California to try her hand at writing for radio, at which she had been very successful in New York. It hadn't worked out to her satisfaction, and she had been packed to return to New York when she heard over the radio about the train, its trip, and the people on it. When she heard my name, she decided to come.

After my divorce, Florence and I were married.

Many couples find they have to go through a period of adjustment when they marry. That was not the case with Florence and me. Our tastes in almost everything have been amazingly alike; conversation has never been difficult; there is always something to talk about. We pick up each other's thoughts, I being mostly the receiver, she being the strong sender. There has always been a "knowing."

When we went back to New York in 1953, there was a strained period when it seemed the whole thing might be over with us, and we parted again. I returned to California to see if I could revive my sagging career, and after a couple of months got started in pictures again. I called Florence, who was reluctant at first, but she finally gave in and we were reunited. In early 1964 we both experienced a deeply emotionally disturbed period and sort of blew our collective minds at the same time; Florence flew off to Mexico and got a divorce. We were parted again, but six months after the divorce we were remarried.

There is a reason for this biographical rundown, for the detailing of the times our lives have touched, separated, and touched again.

Through a friend I was guided to my first astrologer. I called and gave her the necessary information on me, without giving my last name. The reading was interesting, indicating the arts, show business, acting. But it also showed that I was strongly inclined to writing, that it would be the big thing in my life. She studied the astrological chart for a while, looked quizically at me, and began telling me what she saw. She felt I'd committed suicide in a former life, that I'd come back into this life to learn not to commit suicide, and that in a few years I would once again be doing the thing I had been doing when I'd committed suicide in that former life. (All through this life, since I was a youngster, thoughts of knocking myself off have never been far away—in fact damned close to the surface. I still have them, but I've learned to live with them.)

Florence was so fascinated by my reading that she called and set one up for herself. She took along my chart and—after the woman had finished reading for her—she asked how our two charts compared. The astrologer became excited. According to her, our charts indicated that we'd known each other in many lifetimes! In fact we were brother and sister in one lifetime—the charts are that hooked up, practically paralleling one another. Each chart is one half; together they form the whole. She even remarked "You knew one another the moment you met, on first sight," and she added, "You couldn't get away from each other, although your charts indicate many separations, you are Karmically bound."

Florence began studying astrology almost immediately, and in the past few years has become an excellent reader. Making a chart is relatively simple, but reading it correctly takes years of experience, and it does help if the reader can pick up psychically, a gift Florence has. Florence doesn't believe she's particularly psychic, but beginning in 1964, she had some unusual experiences that she admits could be called paranormal or supernatural.

According to Florence, "The first one was quite simple; it started as a dream. Normally I don't remember my dreams, probably because of a very strong psychic censor, but when I awakened from this dream it was as if I had seen or been a party to an actual living experience. It consisted of my contemporary self, dressed in today's clothing, walking through the upstairs level of what obviously was a very rich man's home—not a castle, but a magnificent manor house. Somehow I seemed to know it was in England, although I've never been across the Atlantic. The wainscoting on the walls was of dark walnut, beautifully bas-reliefed—the kind of wainscoting you see in today's better custom homes, with the raised center panel and the beautiful borders. Simple, not ornate, but very rich. This upstairs floor consisted of many apartments, but as I ascended to the top of the stairs, I turned sharp left to a familiar door.

"As I opened it, I saw a very large room with beautiful green carpeting but no furniture, and I heard myself say, 'Oh, they're all gone. Nobody is here anymore,' and I had a very deep sense of sorrow. I didn't go into that room, but instead walked down the very wide hallway and through the other doorways. Instead of opening to single rooms, they were suites of rooms, containing butler's pantries, formal dining room, many bedrooms, kitchens, but no bathrooms.

"The house was evidently built in the era before there was

inside plumbing. As I proceeded through the suites, or apartments, I came to a huge center hall with a square, railed well, which you could look over and see down to the first floor; very much the way the oldtime fancy movie houses in New York used to be. The dream consisted entirely of my touring the whole upstairs of this huge house, or second level. Although each suite was neat and clean—no dust, no cobwebs—there were no wall decorations, no drapes, no furniture of any kind; just the emerald green carpeting. I remember waking up the next morning wishing I could see more of that beautiful house.

"The morning following the next night, after awakening, I realized I had dreamed of the downstairs level of the same manor. The clarity of it remained with me. In those rooms there was ruby red, almost lipstick red, carpeting. The ceilings of both floors must have been very high as I don't remember seeing the ceiling; they must have been way above the normal height. The downstairs dream was not nearly as detailed nor as long-lasting as the dream of the upstairs the first night. I simply entered the main lobby of this house and I was aware of the rooms on either side of the entry hall; they were formal, like a living room, drawing room, perhaps a huge dining room, whatever. But it seemed my main purpose in this second dream was to get up the stairway, a beautiful, wide, curving stairway with satin-smooth wooden balustrade and wainscoted wall. As I reached the top of the stairway, full of eager anticipation, and was turning again to the first familiar door, the dream ended.

"I wondered for a long time just what the dreams meant, and I've never forgotten that house or my feeling for it. Sometime later I was sitting on the guest room bed in my own house, studying. I had my feet up on the bed; I had a manuscript in my lap. I was wide awake. It was early evening and the lights were on. Suddenly, a strange feeling took possession of me. I had the impression I was a young girl about seventeen years old. As I continued to look down at the manuscript in my lap, the feeling changed to one of being real, the pages turned into something else—sheet music, I think it was. The sheets were wider than the manuscript I'd been looking at before. I never did see what was written on the page of sheet music.

"Without moving, I saw hanging over my left shoulder, long, brown, fat sausage curls. I am an older woman, with short dark hair, and I've never had hair the color brown I saw on my shoulder. It was a blonde-brown, actually. I seemed to be wearing a bedjacket of white with little rosebuds all over, and with lace edging. I was in a fourposter bed that had red velours, or some kind of patterned velvet draperies, which were drawn back. There was a light of some kind on a table to my right, and I was sitting on the right hand side of the bed. To my left were two floor-to-ceiling windows, with similar draperies of the same fabric as those on the bed. The ceiling, again, was very high, and this time I thought I saw some gold inlay, or gold paint, or at least gold trim design on it. It was a very big room, and on the wall facing me was again that same wainscoting I'd seen throughout the dreamed-of house. The room's fireplace was in this far wall, but was offcenter, to the left. To the right, on the righthand wall in the corner, was the entry door, in the same location as that familiar door in my dreams.

"Also, I realized I was a cripple. I knew, somehow, that I was sitting in that bed not just because I had gone to bed but because that is where I lived. I knew that I couldn't walk, that I was very young, that I had rather blondish hair and was dressed in the manner I've described, studying some kind of musical manuscript. I was very happy; a tremendous happiness was within me.

"I seemed to be expecting someone to come through that door. And as it seemed the door was about to be opened by that someone, I involuntarily looked up—and of course the whole waking vision, call it what you will, vanished.

"I was sorry about that. Several nights later I was again sitting in the same position on the guest room bed, doing the same type work, and lo and behold, the same vision occurred. I again became this young girl, and I repeated the experience. This time I was very careful not to raise my eyes so I wouldn't break it. I noticed far more detail than I had the first time. But once again, when the moment came for this person to come through the door, the happiness, the expectation, was so great that I involuntarily looked up at where the door would be, and again I lost the vision.

"Somehow, I have the feeling that the man, and I was sure it was a man, was someone I loved very, very much—my beloved, you might say. I also have the feeling that I was a music student and he was my teacher."

Florence's story continues, but it is important to interject some curious confirmations of Florence's memories.

It was about this time that I became interested in having sittings with a number of psychics, mediums, or sensitives, trying to justify in my own mind that there was something valid to all this occult stuff. It seemed the best way was to see what would come out of sittings with psychics to see if any of the information matched. A psychic woman was well recommended, so I called and obtained a sitting with her. During our session she said, "You were a music and dancing teacher in a former life, in England, but you didn't like teaching. You came into this life not liking music or dancing." Music teacher, dancing teacher? Most people like to hear they were Marie Antoinette, Jesus, one of the apostles, or Napoleon. My mother bought a piano for my brother and me when we were young, and when she was out shopping one day I took a pair of pliers and cut all the strings. I like to watch others dance, but I don't dance except when I have to do it in a movie or TV show.

In my book, *Great Ghosts of the West**, I discussed a woman psychic with whom I'd had a number of sittings with amazing results. Florence was so impressed with my first sitting that she called for one, but the woman and her husband were preparing to leave for a vacation so she recommended a woman named Eleanor. Florence received the following reading from Eleanor.

"During one of your previous lifetimes you were a girl in England. You fell from a horse, you were wrongly treated.

* Richard Webb, *Great Ghosts of the West* (Los Angeles: Nash, 1971).

Because of the wrong treatment, you became a cripple." (At no time had Florence mentioned her dreams or waking visions.)

Florence asked "Where did I live in that former life?"

The answer: "In a manor house, not a castle, on the Thames River, and the house is still standing. If you go back to England, you will find it and you will recognize it. You will go into it and remember that you lived there."

Of a second waking experience, Florence said, "It isn't as flattering, but it did happen, and it's part of the overall picture. Lots of people, either in dreams or in a waking state, hallucinate or delude themselves with having been dancing girls, princesses, great military leaders, Cleopatra—you name it. But this next experience I had was a bit of a shocker.

"This happened a few years ago. I had gone to visit a girl friend of mine who had just remarried. I'd never met the new husband, and the visit was partly to see what she'd gotten. It was a very hot summer evening when I walked into their living room. I had no sooner met the husband and sat down when he began to act very nervous. He got up and began to pace around, and made motions as though he was going to leave not only the room but the house. All at once, and it just seemed to slip out, I heard myself saying, 'Joe, you don't have to leave. You don't have to be afraid of me any more!'

"All three of us were rather startled by my announcement. Joe stammered and stuttered for a moment, then sat down. His wife, Norma, laughed and said to him, 'Why in the world should you be afraid of her?' Joe didn't answer. He just sat there looking at me. I answered for him again, involuntarily saying, 'Norma, you see, it's like this. I used to be an executioner, in France, and Joe is afraid of my eyes because all he can remember is a black hood and my eyes shining through. I was an ax-man during the French Revolution, and Joe was a priest. He used to stand on the platform and watch me do the executions. He hated me, but all he knew of my face was my eyes, and that's what he's afraid of now.'

"Norma began to laugh, and she said, 'Joe—a priest? Not

on your life!' As she said that, Joe became even more disturbed, trembling visibly, and said, 'Oh, my God.' I said to him, 'Joe, you wouldn't be nearly as unhappy if you would go back to your faith.' Norma said, 'He's not a Catholic.' Joe crossed himself and said, 'God forgive me, I am.'

"The atmosphere became very strained. We were all embarrassed and startled by what I'd said, and I finally had to leave. While I was talking to them I had the feeling of being a huge man, muscular and swarthy. And, too, while I had been saying those words, it was as though I was looking at Joe and Norma through the eye-slits of a black hood.

"Oddly enough, all my life, I've had an aversion to France and things French. I was a very good student in school, but the one thing I just couldn't master was French and I almost didn't graduate because of it. Yet today I can pick up a piece of French literature and read it, translate it, although I couldn't get a passing grade in school. Just after Richard and I were married, we had an opportunity to go to France on a studio publicity tour. I told him I would go to England, to Italy, but I would not go to France under any circumstances. To this day the idea of going to Paris, the thing most people who visit Europe want to do, is abhorrent to me. I get ice cold when I even think of it—it's something I would least like to do."

Memories of a former life? Or, as is posited by some trance mediums who've had extensive experience in transmitting messages from the other side, perhaps at the time Florence was in Joe's presence, some entity over there, who had in fact been an ax-man during the French Revolution, was present and triggered her to speak as she did. A sort of momentary possession? Who knows?

Perhaps many people have had triggered memories from out of this life, out of the blue, but hesitate to talk about them for fear they will be laughed out of countenance and be called hallucinative or delusional.

4

A Past and Present Life Reading

A popular Hollywood and New York TV performer and master of ceremonies suggested I get in touch with Gregge Tiffen, who was becoming well known in Hollywood as a life reader. Gregge had started out to be a career officer in the army. One night he and his wife attended a seance, and during the session Gregge found he was picking up more answers for the sitters than the entranced medium. Then he began reading everything he could about psychic phenomena. He finally decided he wanted to devote full time to the study of the occult. He applied for a discharge from the army, and his commission as a captain. Within a few months he had his affairs arranged. He traveled to northeastern Tibet and spent the next six years studying in the lamaseries, becoming thoroughly inculcated with the ancient teachings. Upon his return to the United States he made the proper contacts and proved his expertise in the occult sciences. It wasn't long before he was in great demand as a teacher.

The reading he did on me locked in so closely with the

actual facts of my life (the present one, the only one I can remember) that I was truly amazed. "The thing that seems to be most important," Gregge said, "is that lifetimes seem to run in characteristic patterns. Very few people come into just one life experience, learn what they came to do, then drop it and go on to something else. Not in one lifetime. We seem to have certain repetitions in order to learn. We have life patterns, groupings. All of them added together produce the characteristic type of thing that you came in to do this time. You've had some interesting changes, but I will do the characteristic patterns first, and those all group together."

He studied the rectangular chart he'd drawn up, covered with lines, sectioned according to the lifetimes he picked up about me. "Now you weren't these people, but you had a relationship with them—Genghis Khan, Marco Polo, Pope Leo I, and Leonardo da Vinci. You lived in each of those time phases and were either a student of or closely related to the person involved. In each one of those lifetimes one of those individuals became something of a hero to you. As an individual you were lost in each one of those individuals—they could do no wrong. You became terribly insignificant and literally overshadowed by their tremendous power or position.

"In particular, you show a very close relationship to Genghis Khan, so close that you either saved his life or were a member of his family—not a brother but perhaps a relative. You stood in his shadow all of his life, a writer of his exploits. It is quite possible you also had something to do with prompting the historians of the people the khan conquered to write of him so the legends would grow.

"This is also true in the life of Pope Leo I around 450 A.D. Your life then indicates some kind of family relationship, which probably means you were in the official family of the hierarchy, very close to the Pope, his power, and his prestige.

"In these situations you were literally overshadowed by greatness, even though you held positions of worth on your own and could have been reasonably well known. This presents an interesting quirk in the spiritual characteristics—it comes through in this lifetime under any number of guises and any number of lessons.

"Number one, the lesson of how to stand on your own two feet and not live in anybody else's shadow—to do this under such control that you don't go to the other extreme and become too independent, so that nobody can have any empathy with you.

Second, you have to learn the real meaning of greatness. You had a distorted view of greatness. As a child you had a tendency to set up heroes and try to pattern yourself after them. In doing this you lost your own identity, your own personality, your own spiritual characteristics. You lived in a sort of never-never land that kept you from learning who you really are. Also, you lost the sense of goals in life because heroes don't have goals; heroes are the goals. To hold other people in high esteem and awe is another part of the lesson you have to learn. People are people. You hate to see cracks in the veneers of the people you have great admiration for.

"Also, there is a tremendous drive, in this grouping of former lives, to be individually creative. One of the things you suffered badly from, not only in the Genghis Khan life but in both the da Vinci and Pope Leo lives, was the fact that you worked in their shadow and didn't get a chance to create anything on your own. This, by the way, would make you a good actor because you are actually reading what somebody else created rather than creating on your own. Now that you are writing, you are coming closer and closer to understanding that this is the sense and the freedom you need for your own development.

"Interestingly, in this grouping there is no feeling of resentment. You enjoyed working with the great in those lives, and I think you'd still enjoy working with the great. You have no resentment for people who really make it; you don't want them to be weak and fail. There is proof of life when you see a person become successful—the proof is that, if he can do it, he and you are in a locked brotherhood and his gain is your gain. Therefore you like to see people make it—you have a curious lack of resentment."

[This, I feel, is true. This "curious lack of resentment" has often given me pause. There are times when I suffer pangs of envy, but jealousy—the tearing, searing kind of corrosive jealousy that chokes off creative life and actually stultifies the mind and the emotions—hasn't been my bag. Rather, I tend to go the other way and feel inferior and inadequate, despite some personal success. I have always expected other people's success to last but wondered how long it would be before mine crumbled away!]

"Therefore," Gregge went on, "you like to see other people succeed. Everything you saw in the four lives of this grouping you were very proud of. It was as well as if you did it yourself, but that was the problem—you were living an alter ego situation.

"In this lifetime the demand falls primarily in the area of individuality and reality. And one of the things you have to learn in this particular sojourn is the reality of human frailty and the reality of individuality—that no man really works well in another man's shadow. You must step away from all other men and stand in the heat of the sun yourself. At the same time no man is going to be a saint all his life; you have to understand human frailty more as a spiritual thing, as you do human greatness.

"You have two other interesting aspects that come right up on the line of the graph and are being carried through into this present life. One of them was in 42 B.C., in Rome. Most of the gladiators in Rome around that time were slaves. You were in a minor political position in that particular period, and you got caught up in a political subterfuge. As part of the punishment you were sent into the arena as a gladiator—something unheard of because you were a Roman citizen, although not a member of the Senate, but so strong was the opposition to you that the law was stretched and you were thrown into the arena to defend yourself as a gladiator.

"The significance of this life is your tremendous fear of subterfuge—you've got to be told the truth, and you can take it. You have an absolute resistance for anything that's under the table. The spirit has already been hung up badly because of subterfuge—for which you paid a penalty. In this life you had to develop a sense of honesty—a hesitation to be involved or to believe anything of a political nature, especially if it involves a lot of clandestine activities, as is the case with almost everything connected with politics. It makes you see and demand straightforward words and actions.

"You are not a convincing liar! Something like this in your past life would make you an impossible liar. You might try to get away with some lying, but you hate yourself so much and you are so frightened of being caught that it just isn't worth the effort. You just know it won't work out if you lie. Therefore, you just can't deal with people who do lie. Once a person proves dishonest you don't want to believe anything he says or does could be honest.

"Then there is a recent grouping of six lives—from 1400 to about 1805—that never went beyond the age of fifteen. I find patterns like this when I find people who come in from other planets. They touch down, leave, return, touch down, leave, return, until they can adjust to life here, adjust to the vibrations of this planet. In the orientation they come in for a quick, short life, to allow the spirit to adjust to the physical involvement, and then they start the earthly learning process. Even though they've been here before, if they have dwelled on other planets and then returned there is a long period of readjustment. In this life, at around the age of fifteen to seventeen, you could have tried to repeat the pattern of dissolvement, to escape again, but it didn't happen."

[How did he know that? From looking at that chart, upon which were a bunch of apparently meaningless figures, did he see what had happened when I was about seventeen? At that age I developed a cold that degenerated into bronchitis, sinusitis, and then blossomed into a blockage of the tube leading to my right ear, and then mastoiditis. My life hung in the balance for weeks. Now that possible death aspect also shows up in my natal astrological chart. Repeat of a former pattern? Early death?]

"In this period," Gregge continued, "you did a lot of traveling in other galaxies, but it was very necessary that you not break away completely because you were far from finished with this level. There is a tremendous spiritual need, in the area of self-value and independence, to gather information elsewhere. The residue this brings in can be quite odd. You see, we don't know what the spirit has in mind—what its ultimate goal or mission really is. There can be a slight disorientation in the individual. He's here but really doesn't feel this planet is his home and has a sense that there is another place he should be. There is a lack of full orientation to this planet. You feel that almost everything that happens here is damn foolishness. It doesn't have substance, it's childish. You know there is something much better, that humanity is crawling when we should we walking.

"With the lives you have led, both here and previously, you have a sense of impermanency, particularly after a series of such short lives and then embarking on a long life, which you will have in this one, because you've been cut off before. You have the feeling that nothing is going to last.

"We choose our parents, and we choose them for karmic reasons. They are always the opposite of what we come to learn—in order to provide the individual the resistance he needs. One or both of your parents would be a collector of things, stable to the point of never giving anything up, never wanting to move; the extreme of impermanence would be overpermanence. In your case it probably was your mother who was like this."

[Target! Although I was very close to her, my mother's difficulty was her rigidity concerning her own beliefs. Collecting was a veritable passion with her; the thought of losing a personal possession, for any reason, could make her physically ill.]

"Probably," Gregge continued, "the mother would be the type who would say, 'Look at so-and-so. Why can't you be like him? Why can't you do it this way? Why don't you do it my way?' This also directly involves what you came in to do —to learn to strike out on your own, to be an individual, to learn that people are strong and weak at the same time, and not let that destroy your idea about the spiritual good that's involved. More important than anything is to stand in your own spotlight. One of your weaknesses is comparing. Never compare yourself with either the great or the small, but rather say, 'Here I am. I know there are a lot above me, and there are a lot below me, but that isn't important to me.' "

[Target again!]

In 1973, two years after my life reading, a psychiatrist from the Delmar, California, area, who is very well known in the Reichian therapy field (the gestalt therapy system) heard Gregge Tiffen on the radio and was fascinated with his concept of the life reading. He called Tiffen and made an appointment. Then his wife had one. He found the validity so unquestionable that he wanted to explore the possibility of having readings done for his patients to see if they could be used to identify basic problem areas. If this could be done, time spent in discovering and isolating problems could be cut considerably.

The psychiatrist started a program of testing this method and found that it did indeed work. He referred his patients to Tiffen, who did life readings for them, identifying their major problem areas and supplying them with tapes of the readings. In therapy, patient and psychiatrist worked on the problems supplied on the tapes.

The psychiatrist was so impressed with the results from the life reading therapy that he mentioned this approach to some psychiatrists and psychologists in the East. Tiffen went east and worked with them, and they, too, found it an invaluable tool. One commented that without the life reading he feels that everything he is doing with a patient is archaic, that the life reading is really the basis of the psychotherapy of the future—an odd statement for a modern psychiatrist, since the life reading system is so old.

Life readings have been done through the centuries, but we've been so busy "progressing" that we haven't bothered to explore the old systems. Like acupuncture, the system has been in use for centuries, but in the United States we are only now discovering it. However, the life reading has never been used in the way developed by Tiffen and the psychotherapists.

It is only since Tiffen has been doing life readings for patients and for psychiatrists and psychologists, and since he has lectured on the subject at colleges, that there has been a very active interest in the subject. In November 1973 interest had grown sufficiently to prompt a major conference of psychiatrists and therapists to place the subject on its agenda. One of the psychiatrists who has used this method delivered a paper on it, and another appeared on a panel discussion on the subject.

Gregge is convinced that we bring in some learning problems from a former life or lives. Gregge suggests that everyone has at least one problem of some type or another. "What the individual does is build attendant restrictions and blocks around it as the result of his current society and background, upbringing, that sort of thing." The picture that Gregge gives in a life reading is a picture of the lives that are affecting this life, and only the lives that are producing the groundwork or foundation for the current learning experience.

For Gregge to do a life reading, the individual does not necessarily have to be present, but he prefers that they be there because more information can be obtained if there is an opportunity for questions and answers. All he needs about the individual is a name and birthdate, and that's more for his files than for anything else. If a person simply walked in and gave him absolutely no information, he could still produce an accurate life reading.

There is, of course, no way for a person to verify that the problems came from a former life. The only verification comes from the inner response of the individual. Sometimes this response may not come immediately. Gregge cites a specific case that happened in Boston. "I had on my appointment docket that a nun was coming in for a reading. That doesn't bother me. I've done a lot of ex-nuns and ex-priests, and a great many current rabbis. But I was a bit concerned about this current, practicing nun. I gave her the life reading. She was pleasant, but obviously resistant.

"She went back to the psychiatrist who'd recommended it, who happened to be a friend of hers—she wasn't a patient of his. She berated him for having sent her, and she more or less bad-mouthed the whole thing for months. But about six months later, when I was back in Boston, I was talking to the psychiatrist and he said 'Oh, have I got a story for you! The nun left the convent. She came into my office with the tape in her hand and said she was ready to start therapy.' "

PART II
Dreams, Waking and Sleeping

5
I Think I Was Suffocated

Transmigration is not self-evident, proof of reincarnation does pose a problem. Lifelong recurrent dreams, along with momentary or fairly extended waking recollections comprise a bulk of the evidence for the reincarnative hypothesis.

It is not our intent to create difficulties with either science or a religion that denounces belief in reincarnation. But, increasingly, modern man has become more concerned with the supernormal, continuing life, and metempsychosis than would appear on the surface. This is directly attributable to the demands of the younger generation for more concrete spiritual sustenance.

Among my friends and acquaintances is a man of the cloth who has had lifelong recurrent retrocognitive dreams and waking recollections that are indicative of a former life. Although the man, Father Paul, professes doubt in the subject, believing that what he has experienced is precognitive, he did relate the sequences and allowed me to record his story.

I had flown to Oklahoma City after some friends there,

Ron and Sylvia Cahagnet, called and said there was "one helluva ghost" in town, thinking I might like to write it up. (They were aware I was gathering material on "nutty things like that" for a book.) The Cahagnets are a splendid couple of great personal warmth and perspicacity. They met me at the airport, bubbling with news about the ghost. We drove immediately to the house involved and had a four-hour session with the people who lived there. But it seemed the ghost was out to lunch, or haunting someone else at the moment.

That night I stayed with the Cahagnets and slept in an antique solid silver bed (Silver bullets are supposed to be great for laying ghosts, but a whole bed? I guess Ron and Sylvia wanted me to have all the protection possible.) The following day we had lunch at a restaurant where a group of business and professional friends meet once a week to share their experiences, strengths, and hopes with one another. Among others, I was introduced to Father Paul, who sat at our table. The Cahagnets at once told the group what I was in town for, and naturally the good-natured banter took over—the corny jokes, anecdotes about spooks, "hain'ts," and the like. Someone tossed in that each of us had better be careful about the person sitting in the next seat since he might be the reincarnation of a long-dead character come back to bug us. That tossed the napkin on the table for me to casually ask if any of them had even thought they might have lived a former life, had any dreams or recollections about such things? That gave rise to stuff like "Yeah, I was a horse," "I was a lily of the valley," "Ten thousand years ago I was a stone; I remember it well"—and that's about as productive as it got.

After lunch, Ron, Sylvia, Father Paul, and I remained to dawdle over coffee. From Father Paul's demeanor I felt he wanted to berate me or exorcise me on the reincarnation issue. He did neither; he wanted to tell his story. Protestants are in the habit of often addressing their clergy by first names, and I did just that with Paul, without really thinking. After I realized what I was doing, I qualified my getting so personal.

He smiled and said, "I understand. I know you don't mean any disrespect. Call me Paul."

Paul started off by saying that he'd had recurring dreams ever since he was a young boy, dreams that had definite pattern and substance to them, and he would like to tell me about them.

"Understand me, I'm separating my religious order from the story," he said. "All this may be precognitive, as I've been taught. I haven't thought about it too carefully as far as any continuity there might be. During my student days in Texas, when I was trying to make up my mind which religious order would be right for me. I was about fourteen years old, and I was very dissatisfied with the order I was in. I was studying for the priesthood, and members of my order wore a black habit. I've always had a desire to serve, but black is an abhorrent color to me; I don't like black and I don't like to wear it. One day I was visiting a church in San Antonio, Texas, and I saw a brother walk across the sacristy in a brown habit and sandals and a brown scapular. He wasn't wearing a hood. I felt extremely drawn to the habit. I decided instantly that I wanted to be a member of that order. This had such an impact on me that I threw over everything else and joined this particular group. I've stayed with it over twenty years now.

"The second part of the sequence came when I was working in a bank. I was nineteen years old, and one of the sisters, my teacher, sent me to see a priest to see if I still had a religious vocation. When I walked in and saw the habit he was wearing, it again had that powerful effect on me. It was the same brown habit, with the capuche, the scapular, and the tunic."

These are, of course, unsubstantiated feelings, difficult to hook up with a reincarnative recollection. But why the strong emotional reaction to the tunic? In addition to these, Paul had recurring dreams that seem to tie in. There have been two of them.

"One dream I kept having as a child takes place in an Oriental or Byzantine or Arab temple," Paul said. "There are carvings on the walls, pillows on the floor, various pitchers and urns sitting around on low tables; there are finely embossed silver lamps hanging from the ceiling. There were members of my order all through the Mideast in the fourteenth and fifteenth centuries, and I know I was an observer, not a participant, in the temple.

"In another gradation of the dream I saw more. The dream begins with me standing on top of a promontory, or a road paved with very large blue or slate gray, cobblestones, in the evening, after the sun has set. I walk down the road past what appears to be an English castle. It seems to be near a tower. The walls rise straight up, and there is a series of windows fixed in the walls, coming down like a spiral, one below the other. There is also a staircase coming down the outside of the tower. Walking down the staircase is a group of men who look like monks, in brown and white robes. They all have the hoods up on their habits. I can't see their faces, but I can see their beards. As they pass me, they look briefly but don't address me. I have on the full habit of my own order. There is a feeling of great sadness between us, not of hatred or horror but just sadness. It's as though I'd done something wrong, and they are sorry for me.

"In the other dream I kept having as a child, I was in the bottom of a well or deep within a chamber that was like a well. The stones were very large and roughly hewn. There seemed to be no way for me to touch them; it seemed I was bound, with my arms pinned down. There were people looking into the mouth of the well; they seemed to be hooded. I don't know what color the hoods were. The people placed an object over the mouth of the well and went away, and it was black down there. In the darkness I remember trying to climb, but I was bound and kept falling back. I couldn't grab hold of anything. I was helpless. I would cry out, but nobody came. I had a great fear I would suffocate. Then I just seemed to fade away. That recurring dream finally faded about twenty years ago, and I've not had it since.

"In my dreams I've had the feeling that I was rolled up in something, like a carpet or wire mesh, and I couldn't breathe,

Dreams, Waking and Sleeping

and that was how I suffocated. That feeling is so strong that even today I can't stand to have people put their arms around me or cover my mouth in any way. My fear of suffocation is tremendous. It's interesting, because doctors have told me I was born with a stricture of the chest, and you can tell from the way I have been coughing that I still have it. I've been under treatment for it for over twenty years."

With further discussion I learned Paul was born under the sign of Scorpio, which is one of the most interesting signs of the zodiac. Scorpios can go higher than other signs or they can sink to lower depths. Obviously, Paul has gone what is called the Eagle Route; he is a priest, the golden plateau. Billy Graham is a Scorpio; Charles Manson of the Manson Family murders is also a Scorpio, and you can hardly get greater extremes in the higher and lower aspects. Four minutes of difference in time of birth throw two charts a year apart in the individual readings. It could be said that the Graham-Manson charts are *almost* identical—it's that *almost* that made the difference.

Father Paul knew the exact moment of his birth because it had been recorded by his father. I called my favorite astrologer, who can pick up psychically on the person whose chart she is reading. I gave her the five details an astrologer needs to do a good chart: moment of birth, day, month, year, and location. I only said the client's name was Paul—no last name, no other information that might give her the slightest lead. I requested that she put the reading on tape.

I had appointments for story interviews with people in Kansas City, Cleveland, and Buffalo, but two weeks later I was back in Oklahoma City. The tape cassette, which I had asked the astrologer to mail to Ron and Sylvia, was waiting for me. I did not open it but called Father Paul so we could listen to it together.

The astrologer began: "This man, I feel, was a monk in a former life. It is difficult for me to breathe as I read the chart. I feel he was either suffocated or was drowned in a former life. He came into this life with a memory of the way he died. I feel also that he is again a monk. I get it very strongly that in this life he has great difficulty breathing. He feels as if he is suffocating."

Tie that one if you can!

Father Paul went to Rome for the first time about eight months after that reading. He went on an extensive sabbatical and has written me about finding pretty conclusive evidence that some of the things he saw in his reincarnative recollections actually exist.

Here are some of the examples mailed to me from Rome:

September 15: "I've seen the ramps, windows, pits . . ."

September 29: ". . . the Castel Sant' Angelo is only a few blocks from where I'm staying—and it raises the hackles on my neck. It has the elliptical ramp and it has the arches of my dream. It also has the wells in which political prisoners were kept—wells that were meant to serve as receptacles for oil and considered quite horrible as prisons. I have learned that several of our priests were imprisoned there for various reasons . . ."

October 8: ". . . I have found the gray granite slabs and cloistered circular stairway—or at least I think I have."

6

His Transitional Lifetime

We'll call him Kenneth because of some particularly intimate revelations contained in his story, although what he revealed about his present personal life doesn't bear the stigma it once engendered.

Ken was a very successful screen actor in Hollywood for many years. We'd never met until a few months before I obtained this story from him. Hollywood is a relatively small town, yet large enough that even people in the same tight, gregarious business may only meet infrequently, or may never meet, even though they are very aware of each other through publicity, word of mouth, or the screen. My wife, Florence, felt Ken might have a story he would be willing to share with us.

It is possible that we are all of us living transitional lifetimes. Transition is defined as a passing from one condition, form, stage, activity, or place to another. Ken's reincarnative dream recollection of a former life, and his transition in this one, represent the first of their genre I have come upon.

What is really significant about this particular case is that the dream occurred when Ken was two years old. His mother had taken him to Alaska to visit his grandfather, who owned and operated some lumber mills there. Ken woke up crying because of what he had seen in his extremely vivid dream. His grandfather came to his room to comfort him, and Ken told him about the dream.

It wasn't until Ken was six years old that the dream began returning with great clarity, and again when he was in junior high school. When Ken was six, his grandfather sold his lumber mills and moved in with the family. Ken again awakened one night crying because of the dream. His grandfather, who happened to be sleeping in the same room, said, "Men don't cry." Ken remembers clearly telling him, "But Grandpa, I'm not a man in my dream. I'm a lady."

What he'd seen in the dream as a two-year-old was identical in content to the dream he had when he was six. He saw himself as a woman of very commanding bearing and demeanor. The dream setting was a bleak castle. There were cold, gray hallways, and cold, dimly lit rooms. It wasn't a castle filled with a great many people, but there were others there. As the woman, Ken was of average height, slender, fair-skinned, red-haired. The woman had very troubled blue eyes and cried a good deal. It seemed the trouble stemmed from the actions of a handsome man close to her, "perhaps a cousin or even a brother." He was engaged in some undertaking she felt he shouldn't be involved in and she was constantly pleading with him. There seemed to be a war going on, and she seemed to be taking sides between her handsome man and another man, whom Ken never saw clearly. She made a bargain with the handsome man with the understanding that, "if the woman went to bed with the man it would end the war, the bloodshed," Ken recalled. "Sometimes there would be a sexual climax, but it wasn't the climax of ecstasy or joy, it was one of 'sex was on the bargaining table.'"

When the dream occurred, Ken would usually wake up crying, as the woman in his dream had been doing.

When he was in college, Ken went to a psychiatrist to see

if something could be done to explain what was happening. The psychiatrist heard the story in detail and then called in a colleague. They decided to try an LSD experiment with Ken.

Ken describes the results of that session: "When the LSD began to work, one of the psychiatrists told me to go look at myself in the full-length mirror on the wall and describe what I saw. I stepped in front of the mirror and the woman in my dreams appeared to me, clear as a bell. I looked at her for a moment, noting everything about her to the finest detail. Then I turned my head and she did the same thing, same angle. I moved my arms and she moved in unison with me. Then she began to do things on her own, as I watched that mirrored self. I related what I was seeing to the psychiatrists. There *I* was, in the mirror, about thirty-five or forty years old (in my present life at the time I was younger, in college). I was fully dressed in a period costume, and there was nothing disheveled about me. I was a small woman, about five-foot-two, with very refined, delicate features and flaming red hair. My eyes were blazing in fury. While I was watching, the dim figure of that handsome man in all my dreams appeared behind me (the woman in the mirror). I did not turn to look at him, but I did start to cry. Then the woman and the man faded and I was standing there looking at me, Ken, in this life."

The opinions of the psychiatrists are interesting: "The two of them concluded, after the LSD thing was over, that what I had was a masochistic dream, that I was punishing myself in this manner for having feminine instincts and desires, and that going to bed with the man in my dream would somehow end the war in my own life, in which, at this point, I was feeling my homosexuality very keenly. Yet they could never adequately explain my having that same dream when I was only two years old, or six. I'm sure homosexuality didn't bother me when I was two."

Ken today doesn't feel that the diagnosis of the two psychiatrists is correct. He feels they were stumped and came up with their own interpretation, which "they are entitled to, as a theory."

Being an actor under long-term contract to a studio during the 1940s and 1950s, the possibility existed that Ken had been on a movie set that contained sets of the fourteenth or fifteenth century, the period he saw himself in as the woman. But he recalls, "The closest movie set or backlot period buildings that would begin to come close to what I saw in the dream were English castles, but the castle I lived in was not English. I have also questioned myself because I've read Dostoevski, Tolstoi, books on Rasputin and Catherine the Great. But you see, the dream occurred long before I had read any of those, even before I could read, and my folks hadn't taken me to a movie at age two."

Transfiguration

Another facet of Ken's phenomenon is what must be called transfiguration; the transferral or change of the outward form, figure, or appearance. This physical phenomenon has taken place with Ken two times to his knowledge.

The first time it happened, Ken had been drinking heavily. One night a friend—let's call him John—came to the house and had a few drinks with Ken. At one point in the evening Ken went into what John called a "turn-of-the-century flight of fancy." Ken became very elegant, played classical music by the yard, and took on a very dominating, commanding, regal air. Also Ken spoke in tongues (glossalalia). But the most startling thing was that Ken transfigured into a woman right before John's eyes! Not his body—just his face, which became that of a woman. In addition, Ken spoke in Swedish and wrote some lines in Swedish. I asked Ken about the Swedish. He said he'd never studied it, had never even played around trying to speak it, and couldn't understand how he could possibly write it. Ken's grandfather and grandmother were Norwegian, but Swedish was never spoken by the grandparents, nor by Ken's parents. John had taken the writing to the university where he was a student and had it analyzed. It was Swedish.

Ken explained: "John said that while I was undergoing the transfiguration I appeared to be a women in a lot of trouble; that I seemed to a woman of royal blood. Of course I used to laugh about this because you hear about homosexual 'queens,' and he said that apparently I was one, a real one! He said I became physically beautiful, very petite, and in the middle of the transfiguration I cried and sobbed my heart out. From what he could gather, when I was speaking English and crying I kept repeating 'my cousin.' " All of that corresponds with my reincarnative dream. I've come to know in the past couple of years that I was in an alcoholic blackout that night. I had, or have, no memory of what John described; I didn't have any recollection even the day after it happened. I was living the dream, acting it out, with absolutely no conscious knowledge of what I was doing."

A few months after I'd met Ken, my wife and I invited him to the house for dinner. Afterward we sat around the living room, Florence in a chair about five feet to my left, next to a table lamp. I was seated on a small sectional. We were both facing Ken, who had made himself comfortable on the couch opposite us. The lighting from three lamps was subdued, but bright enough to show his face clearly.

I don't remember just what the conversation was at the moment it happened, but Ken was talking quite animatedly. Suddenly his face, which isn't particularly lean or plump, began to change. (Though Ken is a homosexual, he is definitely masculine in appearance.) His facial skin seemed to be tightening up, his nose thinned at the bridge and nostrils, his features became delicate and refined. In just a few short moments he became, facially, a beautiful woman!

I shot a glance at Florence, who in turn was glancing at me questioningly. We both saw the transfiguration at the same time. We didn't say anything, just watched. After about a minute Ken's face began to relax, and in a few moments it had returned to its male aspect. Florence and I still didn't say anything to each other or to Ken, but it had made quite an impression.

About twenty minutes later it occurred again—the transfiguration to a beautiful woman, then back to the male face. A look at Florence and I noted she had seen this one, too.

I'd previously read about transfiguration and had watched it occur when I was sitting and talking with noted medium Arthur Ford in his hotel room in New Haven, Connecticut, when he was working on his last book. At the time of Ken's transfigurations I didn't know him well enough to question him about it. Only after I'd asked Ken about a possible reincarnative story and we were discussing transfiguration incidents did I tell him what had happened at my house.

When I asked Ken if he could recall at what age he began to feel this could be a transitional life for him, he answered: "There has never been any conflict in my own mind that I was more feminine than masculine. There was only the conflict of trying to tell other people and their refusal to accept it. I have always admitted and defended my femininity. When I expressed this to my grandfather, his counsel was that if I was indeed feminine I would be protected by spirits unknown to me. He listened to me recount my dream many times. He never laughed at me, and he wasn't shocked. Everyone else went over backward and told me it couldn't be true, that I would outgrow it and change. I think Grandpa knew enough about mythology and history not to scoff at the concept of reincarnation.

"It was when I was about fourteen or fifteen that I came to the definite conclusion that I was the reincarnation of the woman in my dreams. I felt I shouldn't have been a male in this lifetime, that it was a mistake—or if it wasn't a mistake I would be female in my next life and was in a transitional period. You know, frequently when I was young my grandfather would look at my throat and say, 'You have a swan throat.' That pleased me very much, although I've never thought much about looking like a swan!"

When I asked Ken his feelings about falling in love, he replied: "You mean is it different from a man falling in love with a woman? I don't think there is any difference. I have an emotional, spiritual, and physical attraction to someone—

and I'm speaking from my own feminine point of view, you understand. I feel I am that woman of my dreams, although in this life I have not bargained as she did. A fantastic thing happened to me a few years ago. I'd gone to a party at a large house in Hollywood. There were at least a hundred guests. I saw a man I'd never seen before in this life and knew nothing about until we were introduced. He was the image of the 'handsome man' from my dream. There was immediate recognition by both of us. We lived together for about two years, during which time he was awarded the Nobel Prize, for what I won't tell you. Two years later he died. He was not my brother or my cousin in this life."

7

What Was It?

There was a period in my early quest for reincarnative experiences and/or recollections during which I literally went from door to door in my neighborhood asking if anyone had something they could relate. My wife and I have lived in our house for many years, so I wasn't a complete stranger wandering around asking nutty questions, although I will admit that a couple of neighbors, when questioned, rebuffed me in no uncertain terms, leaving no doubt they wanted me to shove off.

One neighbor, Miriam, did have a "sort of funny thing happen," and she wanted not only to relate it but get my views on what I thought of it. It is definitely in the dream category (waking and sleeping), and if the first one isn't a reincarnative recollection it could be precognitive of a scene that she would see in an interesting manner two years later.

"It started as a dream at first, but later I would, even awake, catch a glimpse of what seemed to be a memory of driving down a wide dirt-packed road, which I seemed to know was a main thoroughfare, in a countryside area. The right side of the road was bordered by a very tall, dense hedge, about ten feet high, that grew right along the edge of the road and went as far as the eye could see. To the left the hedge was shorter, about four feet high, and beyond this hedge I saw out of the corner of my eye, as it were, lawns with trees here and there and medium sized houses, or cottages, irregularly spaced about an acre apart, in the distance. I was driving one of the early model autos and was dressed in the kind of driving habit one sees in pictures of the first motorists, perhaps around the turn of the century or shortly thereafter.

"As I neared a narrow dirt road that turned off to the left, the steering wheel seemed to turn by itself in my hands, toward that road. I struggled to keep on the main road, but the wheel had a mind of its own! And the auto and I went down the narrow lane. Here the houses were smaller, closer together, and one in particular was so set on its site that the corner of it touched the road's edge while its sides made a 45 degree angle to the road. Again the wheel took over and I crashed the car into the projecting corner of the house. The dream or vision ends with my knowing I have been thrown from the driver's seat; I am lying on the ground and there is a circle of faces looking down at me, and the dream ends.

"About two years after I had the first of these recollections I went to see a film made in Norway, and halfway through the picture I was startled to see, on the screen *the same road,* with the same hedge, the same landscape and types of houses, and as the camera took us down the main road, it passed my side road and I found myself shrinking back into my seat in fear that it was going to go down that little narrow road, but it did not, so I didn't see if the triangular house corner was still there. What it did do was tell me where my past experience had taken place, and somehow that seemed to put the memory to rest and I haven't had either the dream or the waking vision since then."

Was the recollection reincarnative, or precognitive? It could possibly be both.

In the second experience Miriam and some friends were sitting in her living room watching a television documentary showing various methods used by the fire department to rescue people from burning buildings. The fire was simulated, the firemen were being used as actors, the picture was not part of a melodrama, and it made no attempt to invoke emotions, being educational and informative only.

"Halfway through the show there was a scene of a mother throwing her baby out of a window into a fireman's outstretched arms. Suddenly my chest felt as if it would burst. I broke out into loud uncontrollable sobs, I was hardly able to breathe, and I experienced such an immediate feeling of grief as I have personally never known. My guests were really startled (*shocked* would be a better word), but not as much as I. Just as suddenly the real me seemed to be standing apart, looking on in amazement at this sobbing, grief-racked woman. After a few minutes I was able to control myself, but the feeling of deep heartbreak stayed with me for a long time.

"I have no children, have never had or lost a baby, have never really had a desire to have children. When this incident occurred, I *knew* that sometime, somewhere, I had been a mother who had gone through the horror of a fire and at that time I had to throw my baby out of a window in the hope of saving its life. It is impossible to prove this, I know, but it was so real to me that I *know* it was a recall of something just like that which I had been part of, and not in this life."

8

Kiyo

Kiyo, a girl with sloe eyes, long, dark brown hair, beautiful smile and confident manner, is Eurasian. Her father was Japanese, a dentist in Boston; her mother was American born, of Scots-English extraction. Kiyo is short for Kiyoko, which means "pure running water." She is an esoteric astrologer. *Esoteric* is defined as "hidden, taught only to a select number, not intended for the general body of disciples," as opposed to *exoteric*, that which is outside and exposed to the public, which is how most astrologists read charts.

Kiyo showed up on the arm of Jess Stearn, author of *The Search for the Girl with the Green Eyes* and other books on the supernormal. Jess was doing a new book dealing with some phases of astrology and was getting research material from Kiyo. They rounded out the group of eight at our table in a restaurant in Sherman Oaks, California. The occasion was the monthly "Sun Sign" dinner get-together of noted astrologers, students, and those knowledgeable in parapsychology and the occult. The wife of a top Los Angeles official was present, in company with her friend, a well-known woman psychologist.

During the cocktail hour before dinner I managed to learn the following information from Kiyo: She was born in this country. At an early age she went to Japan and was educated in a school conducted by Canadian teachers. Her psychic abilities developed at an early age. Recollections of former lives have been constant with her for years. She has done astral projection (out-of-body travel) frequently. After becoming an astrologer she found she could pick up on the person being read for, and thereby go deeper into the natal chart, so she entered the field of esoteric astrology.

When I told Kiyo the subject of this book, she handed me her card and asked me to call her when I had a chance because she might possibly have something that would interest me. When I called upon the lovely lady, this is what she told me:

"I started having very special dreams at a very young age. I was aware when I had them—at ages six, seven, and eight—that they were not just the ordinary type of dreams. They were different from the dreams you can logically relate to daily events. Because I had so many reincarnative dreams as a child, I didn't think it was anything that special. My recollections have stayed with me, losing no detail, year after year.

"I had another very impressive dream experience. In that dream I found myself walking alone in what appeared to be the desert. The sky was semidark—not so dark you couldn't see anything, though. I could see my destination as I walked to it. It was the very majestic stone wall and gate of an ancient walled city. It was impressed upon me that the color of that wall was definitely a reddish-brown. I remember making particular note of that. There were a number of people streaming in and out of the gate. It was extremely busy and large, and seemed to be a merchant city. Everybody was on foot, carrying goods piled high on their shoulders, bundles on their heads.

"I was me doing the looking and the walking, but I was dressed in baggy clothes, dark in color. I was carrying a bundle and I could feel its weight. I don't know what was in it, but I know I took good care of it because I had the feeling someone might steal it if I didn't hold onto it. I was a merchant, definitely.

"As I walked through the gate and into the city, I spoke to people or they spoke to me—as you do in a small town. I was about eighteen when this dream happened. In the dream I was a man of about forty."

Kiyo also took me into another experience she had during the same time period:

"A boy and I were running, and I knew for a fact that he was my brother, and I knew we were in the Orient. I had quite a number of Oriental dreams about my past lives over there. I felt this one was in India. We were street urchins— not the grandiose princesses, holy men, and kings so many people conjure up for themselves as their former lives. I was an urchin girl, pure and simple. I was dirty and was looking desperately for food. We both were, my brother and I. I was about eleven or twelve, and we were so dirty it was hard to tell the difference between us. I was older than my brother. We must have done something wrong, because I remember we were running for our lives and there were people chasing us, screaming at us. We were running on a double street—a main street that was higher up with another street lower down on the same parallel. We were both very scared and were crying. This must have been an actual experience, because it left such a deep, painful impression.

"As we were being chased, we ran down off the street and along a river bank. There was shrubbery growing alongside it. Although I didn't go right up to the edge of the water, I was aware of its existence and I knew my way around completely. I was totally familiar with the surroundings. I knew we didn't live right there by the river. We were some distance from our own home and I wondered if we would ever get back to it.

"We ran and hid in some shrubbery, but it was too late. The people chasing us hauled us out of our hiding place and began beating us while they took us back toward the street.

I felt the beating so vividly that it awakened me and I was crying my eyes out. The recollection of that former life incident has never left me.

"There was another reincarnative dream. When I told my parents about the dreams, they just smiled. In this one I lived in a desert area, in what can only be called a skin house—a tentlike dwelling made of animal skins. I have the feeling I was a male in that life. This time I was also an urchin. In this recollection I was reliving the experience of watching a huge structure being built. This huge, round, gigantic piece of architecture was going up, and we kids would sit on the wall and on the sand and watch the men build it, day after day, year after year. As time went on, in the dream, I would go back and see the progress of the building (and I was growing physically all this time). I could see the change from being a child to being a young adult, then middle-aged. This all happened in one dream, and it seemed to span many, many years.

"I watched the workmen finally work on the demi-relief that was placed around the structure. The demi-relief was of hunters with animals that looked like antelope. The antelope were harnessed to what appeared to be a carriage or chariot.

"Later, in the last part of the dream when I went back to see what they had done to the demi-relief, the antelope were all painted. The whole demi-relief was in brilliant blue, and I thought that was rather peculiar. I found out later that the Egyptians were the only people who were able to concoct that deep, vibrant, cerulean blue, and to this day some of it has remained on various Egyptian artifacts. It was extremely lasting, and noted for its intensity and brilliance.

"Another thing that amazed me was that, despite the sandy terrain and the brilliant sun, which normally would be extremely hot, I never got the feeling that the heat was that extreme. We hear today that Egypt is very hot and dry, but it wasn't like that in the days I am talking about.

"In another dream of that period, and about the same area, I was walking alone over beautiful meadowland where the grass was quite high. It wasn't like cropped grass only a few inches high, or even pastureland that has been grazed by animals. The grass was almost waist- and, at times, eye-level height.

"I walked up a hill and came to a very beautiful lake. Reflected in it was a fantastic snow-white structure. This apparently was nothing new to me because I accepted it without question or amazement and proceeded to walk toward it. The building was so gigantic that when you got up to it you couldn't see either end of it. It looked like an enormous palace. There were literally hundreds of steps leading up to the top of it, and I had to sit down before reaching the top. The weather was temperate and there was a cool breeze.

"The structure I was climbing was one of the Pyramids, and it was faced or covered with white marble. At one time the Pyramids were faced with white marble, but they were pillaged over the ages until all that remains is what we see today. I'd never been told that, but this was my recollection when I returned to that former life. When the Pyramids were built, that one anyway, the whole country, the weather—everything was different from the way it has been for thousands of years.

"I have also had one recollection that has to do with another planet. This wasn't a dream but a light trance. I'd been practicing meditation, and I fell into a light trance. I wasn't frightened. I remember being just a wee bit lonely on that other planet. I was intrigued by the pure beauty and the adventure of it, and that emotion overwhelmed any anxiety I had. I found myself walking along a very wide river bed. The gravel or sand I was walking on was just like fine beach sand, but this was not a beach. I would say the river bed was about a mile wide; it was not a little river. There was a gentle slope on the bank I was nearest to, and I noticed the stones were larger, as though they had been pushed out of the way by the action of water rushing down the middle of the bed. The air was extremely clean and clear.

"Along the way I saw what appeared to be a group of buildings set about a mile apart. They looked from a distance as if they were made of mother-of-pearl, done in freeform sculpture. I remember marveling at a particularly tall structure, at its size and great beauty and the way the mother-of-pearl texture glistened. The buildings didn't seem strange to me—I knew what they were. There were what appeared to be round holes punctured through the outside of the structure.

"I walked from the river bed up the bank, went over to one of them, and just stood there looking at it close up. Those structures were actually gigantic clams! They were set on end, the base embedded in the ground and the other end projecting up at least fifty to sixty feet into the air. If those clams were sitting on end, it would suggest that at one time this whole area had been under water, possibly under a sea, and as the water receded the wind and water took all the debris from around them and left them upended the way they were. The wind was blowing through those round freeform holes and it was a beautiful sound, almost as if it had been orchestrated.

"I felt I was going to meet my father, that further on up was a city or town where he lived—that my family was there and I would meet my father. I wasn't in a strange or alien land. This dream sequence happened when I was about twelve years old. My own father was very much alive at the time, but in my dream my father, on the other planet, was someone else, another man.

"There were tree stumps on that planet; they weren't alive and flourishing—they were petrified stumps, highly polished by the action of the sand and the wind, the way the glacial rocks have been polished by the wind and water in Yosemite National Park. The first time I saw them, they immediately put me in mind of the ones I'd seen—different, yet the same.

"I'm not claiming this planet *was* Neptune, but the feeling was that of Neptune. I don't know if Neptune has any water on it now, but if that's where I was in that life it was a dying planet, dying from lack of water.

"This next was one of the later dreams. It was in the fall about eight years ago. I went to Death Valley with my former husband. We got there late in the afternoon, went through the museum, looked things over through the telescope outside.

Dreams, Waking and Sleeping

Being very tired, I ate dinner and went to bed. Even though I'd seen some things in the museum and looked out over the valley, I don't believe that what I dreamed could have had any bearing on what I'd seen. The dream was detailed, in color, and I was back there in another life. The place where we were staying is called Wildrose Junction. There are lodges for rent and a restaurant.

"Death Valley is probably one of the most desolate places I've ever been, but there is a stark beauty about the place that is haunting. There is nothing but mountains, sand and rocks, and strange formations.

"This dream recollection shook me to my very timbers. When I awoke in the morning, I said, 'I can't believe it. I can't possibly believe it.' I made my husband go with me and we walked the whole area while I talked my dream. I had been there before!

"I don't know how many thousands of years ago it was. I pointed out over the whole area and told my husband that this area had at one time been a beautiful sea—not a lake but a sea. There had been a number of small islands rising right near the mountain where we were, and the place where we were standing had been an island at one time. The water had been, like most sea-water, salt.

"I was an American Indian. Unlike what we are given to know about the Indians, living in tribes with a few here and a few there, this was a booming city, an extremely progressive city. In my dream I was walking up a very steep street—like walking up a hill. It wasn't so steep that people couldn't walk up; it was more like the steep streets in San Francisco, made of hard-packed dirt, but not as wide as our city streets. The people were red-skinned and rather small in stature. Actually, we were more a yellow-red; this I remember distinctly.

"I was a child, running up and down the street. People were walking back and forth, carrying shoulder poles of merchandise—not the yoke type of the Far East but carrying the poles over their shoulders with baskets hanging from them, front to rear. Most of the men were not wearing anything from the waist up. They had on what appeared to be a sort of knee-length short skirt, with a border design—a bit like Swastika patterns. I have the definite feeling that we were Aztec Indians—I don't know how we got there, but there we were, and flourishing. There were many trees about—a lot of greenery.

"I had no feeling that we were a wild or pugnacious people. We were interested in commerce, trade, fishing, some agriculture, and we were a happy people. The temperature was hot, but not unbearable the way it is now, and there was a nice breeze blowing. Later, when I read up on the known history of the area, I was amazed to find that there were fossil shells, bones, and fish skeletons of every kind that live in ocean salt water. In my dream I saw the body of water. And we had bicycles! They didn't look like bicycles we have today, of course, and we had carts with big wooden wheels."

Kiyo didn't know it, but Indians have been found buried in caves above what was once the water line in that area. The Indians buried their dead sitting up in vases of oil, and caves with the vases containing the Indian mummies have been and are being found even today. The culture dates back fifteen thousand years, to a time when that area was lush and subtropical.

9

They Called Me
Gracias a Dios

Richard Dunn was born and reared in England, and he possesses that most attractive British accent and the inimitable English bearing of reserve, detail, and correctness. I met Richard at a party in the San Fernando Valley. One of the guests in our group asked me how my manuscript on reincarnation was coming along; Richard overheard the remark and said he had a reincarnative recollection I could use if I wished to. Here it is as it was related to me.

Richard began: "My last name was Fonseca in the life I lived from 1691 to 1772, a span of eighty-one years. I've never remembered what my first name was then, but the natives called me by a nickname—Gracias a Dios. I guess they meant Thanks to God, Fonseca, or Thank God for Fonseca. I was a Spaniard, and most of my adult life was spent in the jungles of Colombia—not far from Panama City, actually. I was interested in emeralds—I still am—and there were plenty of them in the area where I settled. I've always had a great love for the beauty of emeralds, and whenever I see one

I try to get its history. The first time I ever heard of the emerald mine in Muzo, in Colombia, it rang a bell. I could actually see the place in my mind's eye—it triggered memories that are quite real to me, and the mental pictures I have of that life have come into focus more and more as the years go by. Sometimes the waking scenes are augmented by dreams that have mixed in to give me a more complete overall picture.

"Usually the aborigines drove the white man out because of the shameful way the early Spaniards, like Francisco Pizarro, massacred them in the search for treasure. I established and maintained honest relations with the Indians and they allowed me to stay on. They were quite poor in that area in the 1700s, and would practically give the emeralds away for food, so dishonest people had gotten out with enormously valuable gems, giving the natives only a fraction of their worth—or just outright stealing them.

"The natives down there were a bloodthirsty lot when they were aroused. They warred against other tribes mostly, and they were quite adept at cutting off the heads of their enemies and shrinking them down to a size little larger than a baseball.

"To pinpoint the area I'm talking about—and these memories, as I say, came back to me over a period of three or four years—I obtained some historical data and began reading up on the country to see if the things had happened as I was seeing them. We can use Panama City as the starting point and trace along the Pacific coast toward the frontier of Colombia up to the headwaters of a river called the Rio Sambu. That is the area—and you notice I haven't said 'the exact area,' because I don't want some booby treasure hunter heading off down there and perhaps getting his head shrunk. Even though it is against the law now, the natives will shrink a head or two, just to keep their hand in.

"As people who've been in the Panama-Colombia area know, the tides are something to marvel at. When the tide is rising, you can ride the sixteen-foot swell for forty miles; then suddenly it just quits and starts running back out again, just as fast, and your boat is left stranded on dry land. In that former lifetime I hired Panamanian boatmen to ferry us along the coast and up the Rio Sambu. They were scared and it was only by offering them much more than they could make otherwise that we got them to go along.

"The river wasn't large, but it was filled with alligators and it wasn't at all safe to bathe in it unless you were ready to risk your life. I don't remember just how I met the Indians who lived there, but somehow we managed to make an impression on them with presents of various kinds and they allowed us to stay, sort of on probation. After all I was a hated Spaniard. We were taken first to a village along the Rio Sambu. After they had established that I would be honest with them, they brought me some presents in return for those I'd given them. One was a beautiful emerald. There was a lot of gold about—they wore it as amulets and had rings of solid gold in their noses—but when I mentioned the gold they shut up and became really guarded, and I dropped the subject. Yet they didn't hesitate to give me the emerald.

"From then on, in my dealings with the Indians, I tried in every way to show them I was on their side and had their best interests at heart—and I did, you know. Finally they began taking me out into the jungle on hunting trips with them, and it was during one of those trips that I found out where the emeralds came from. There was a huge area on a mountainside, and the stones were on the surface as well as underneath the ground.

"I'm sure that if I went back there right now I could, by talking with the people of the area and the natives, relocate the mines where I operated in that former life as Gracias a Dios Fonseca. The name Fonseca would also be found in written documents in Panamas City, if they are still intact. One day I will go to Panama City or get in touch with the officials through whom I can make the necessary inquiries. This memory has intrigued me since I was a youngster—and the feelings and recollections are growing stronger as I get older. It isn't an obsession—just something I have to check out in order to convince myself. The memory pictures are so crystal-clear. I know it sounds like something right out of a grade B movie, but it's true as I've related it to you—and it's correct in the details.

"Also, most people are bothered by mosquitos and bugs, but I've never been. In those mental image pictures of living in the jungles in the 1700s I was never bothered by the clouds of mosquitos or bugs. I have seen myself walking the jungle trails without any covering of any kind while other white men with me are loaded down with netting and ointments for protection against insects.

"Also, during that same period, I got up around the Colombian coast above where the Panama Canal was finally constructed and had some dealings with the San Blas Indians. They live on numerous islands off the coast of Colombia. The San Blas moved there after Pedrarias, called The Cruel, massacred two million of them in eighteen weeks while he and his men were plundering for gold. The first time I ever saw a San Blas Indian, in New York, I knew instantly that I had been with people like him before, and I knew where he came from. Not specifically, you know, but I just knew he had come from around the Panama-Colombia area, which proved to be true when I spoke with him. I've never been a dedicated student of the history of the races on this planet, although, having been raised in England, I can usually tell where various people come from on the continent from the way they look. My knowledge of the rest of the planet's people is very limited. I'm not even an amateur anthropologist.

"I died there in Colombia. Not violently, but more with my boots on, working perhaps—a natural death. No fighting was involved. There has never been a frightening or distasteful memory of my life there. I believe it is even possible that I might be taken to my own grave there in Colombia—that's how strong the knowing is with me.

"I don't wish to turn the research of my former life over to other people because I don't know how well I could trust them. They might get on the trail of the emerald treasure, take the bit in their own teeth and go into the jungle—and it's quite possible they also might not come out. That has happened to many whites, even recently. They try to get into the jungles by conniving and lying about what they are after, and then they get gold- and gem-crazy and wind up missing. I saw a white man's shrunken head in the museum in New York and it had come from the very area we are talking about—recently, too, within the last fifteen years."

Richard Dunn didn't stop with the recollection of that lifetime, but other memories of lives he'd lived weren't as pronounced in definition. One remembrance he has deals with a period when he was a member of the College of Cardinals in Rome, during the reign of Pope Gregory I. Richard's name at that time was Capité. He remembers his rebelliousness during those days, and bringing a good deal of censure down on himself because of it. The church had fixed itself rigidly, and Capité bucked under the yoke. One thing he didn't like at that time was fixing the mass in Latin—crystallizing it for the ages using a "dead" language.

Just a few years ago, when Richard and his family were living in England, they visited Rome for the first time. They took a tour of the Vatican, like all tourists. He describes the experience:

"When we were in the Vatican, it was really weird. I was walking up the steps. Usually there were a lot of people around, but right at this moment I was alone, going up toward the huge room at the top of the steps. Suddenly I felt a sort of hushed silence. I received the distinct impression of myself in a white robe, with a certain type of priestly hat on. It felt very normal and natural, and as I got to the top of the steps I saw all the people in the big room looking at the altars and things, and I knew they were waiting for me."

Richard laughed as he added, "A sort of 'I shall be with you in a moment' type of thing. When I got to the others, I had to shake myself out of the reveries I was in to speak to them and call their attention to my presence so we could proceed from there, under my direction. Nothing in that room was strange or new to me. I'd seen it all before, could discuss the objects with a great deal of knowledge and intimacy, yet I'd never been there before, nor had I seen pictures of the particular objects we looked at. People were asking each other questions about various things, and I found myself telling them where they could find such-and-such in that huge room."

Richard also has been party to or has witnessed paranormal experiences that have nothing to do with reincarnation and so have no place in this book. Those occurrences have been recorded and will no doubt show up in future writings of his own, or by another author to whom he will relate them. In January 1974 I received a call from Richard; he was returning to England, gave me his address, and insisted we keep in touch.

PART III

Time-Tripping and Projection

10

He Lived in the Fourth and Nineteenth Centuries

Reverend Tony Benik sat very calmly as he began telling me that when he was about seven years old his grandmother noted that he possessed psychic gifts. He would tell some people who came to the house that certain things were going to happen to them, and sometimes those things would happen within hours after he'd predicted them. Even though his grandmother was a Roman Catholic, she called herself a white witch. She tried to help Tony develop his psychic abilities. While in school he noticed that, if he didn't do his homework, he seemed to know the answers the next day when he needed them. I asked him if he slept on a book, as the American mystic Edgar Cayce did. He answered that he had not done it, hadn't known anything about that method. As a matter of fact he hid his book because he hated homework and hated schoolwork. He liked to play too much. When the nuns found out he didn't study, they used to give him a bad time—they'd rap him over the knuckles or give him extra homework to do, which he never did anyway because he always knew the subject, whatever it was. So why should he study?

I asked Tony if he had total recall memory.

"I wouldn't say that. I picked up what the contents of a book would be. I just seemed to know the details of what the book was about."

He learned concentration: "The first thing my grandmother tried to do with me was to develop my concentration. I did develop a very strong power of concentration because of her training, and I've always thanked her for it. I can concentrate on one thing and knock out everything else; my mind will be centered only on the exact thing I want it to focus on. Grandmother taught me to use the cards in this manner. I would put them in a square formation—a card in each upper corner, a card in each lower corner, and card face up in the center. Then I would throw everything from my mind, just concentrate on that center card, and say whatever came to my mind.

"I remember one lady, a very good friend of grandmother's from Philadelphia. She didn't believe in psychic gifts or card reading. Grandmother finally got her to sit with me and see if anything came through my concentrating on that center card. I didn't know what I was actually saying when I did the reading for her, telling her things that were coming through to me, but do you know what—she fainted! She was a great big woman—I would say she weighed about two hundred pounds—so when she fell off her chair the whole floor shook. I was so scared I got up and ran out of the house!

"Grandmother brought the woman to somehow, and then got me back in the house to continue the reading. I didn't want to do it. Every time I would say something and the woman would gasp or roll her eyes, I would get up and start for the door. I would talk in English, but the woman and my grandmother had been born in Lithuania and they would talk in Lithuanian. I didn't know what they were saying. The woman could understand English but couldn't speak it well. I'm a first-generation American, but I can only speak a few words of Lithuanian and understand very little more.

When I finished the reading, the woman seemed very happy; she kissed me and gave me fifty cents. That was a lot of money in those days, and I mentally counted the candy and ice cream cones I could buy all week. That was my first experience in doing a reading for someone outside the family.

"Then there were a lot of Catholic priests, monks, and missionaries Grandmother would invite to the house. I would do readings for them and they would bless me like crazy. I was the most blessed kid in the whole neighborhood.

"This was when I was between the ages of eight and twelve. I have to mention a story here because my grandmother was a paradox. I used to wonder how she could be spiritual, living the Catholic religion in everything—and yet she made bathtub gin! She installed a bathroom in a closet right off her bedroom so she could make the gin and still use the tub for bathing. I remember one rather warm day when I felt like cooling off. The tub looked as though it had water in it, so I shucked off my clothes and stepped in. It was cold, too. I had just started to squat down into it when my grandmother came charging in. She grabbed me and yanked me straight up out of the tub, shaking me furiously so very drop would come off. Then I noticed two men standing behind her. They told her, 'We don't pay the full price—the kid's had his can in it.' Grandmother said, 'He's a virgin, so the price is double!' That is the way she was. I don't know whether she got the double price, but I roar every time I think about it.

"Grandmother tried to get me to read a crystal ball. I just thought it was a great big marble and tried to snitch it so I could show the other kids I had the biggest marble on the block. I never could read a crystal ball. One day we were sitting and she was trying to get me to read the ball, but I kept looking at a glass full of water on the table. She saw what I was doing and asked if I saw anything. I did; I saw faces—not large ones but small ones.

"She asked me if I recognized any of them. I told my grandmother one of them was the face of the woman across the street from us. She looked sad, her mouth all drawn down at the corners. Grandmother wanted to know why she looked sad. I just came out with 'David has broken his leg.' I had seen David only a couple of days before that, but he didn't have a broken leg. However, when my grandmother checked on it, it was true.

"Grandmother began working on me to see if I could get impressions from holding an object in my hands. Later I learned it's called psychometry—my grandmother didn't even know the name for that kind of divining. She would put an object in an envelope, seal it, and hand it to me to read. I thought it was kind of silly to have the things in an envelope because I could tell what they were.

"I remember once she had me hold a man's wallet in my left hand and tell her the impressions I got. The moment I touched that wallet my hands started to burn; it was hotter than a firecracker. I started to tremble and then to cry. I told her I didn't want to hold it, but I found I couldn't even open my fingers to release the wallet. She asked me to tell her what I was feeling, and I told her about the burning, almost as though the wallet was on fire. She got excited and wanted to know what kind of fire. I had tears running down my face, but she made me sit there and tell her what I was getting.

"The burning sensation ran clear up to my shoulders and out across my chest. I told her I smelled burned hair; I could smell fire. She told me to close my eyes and tell her where the fire was. Suddenly I seemed to become the owner of the wallet and I said, 'I'm in the bedroom—the whole bed is on fire. I was asleep and I woke up. The first thing I did was reach for the wallet and get up and run.'

"She wanted to know if I could smell flesh burning. I didn't know what burning flesh smelled like, but I told her I smelled a very sweet odor and she told me that was burning flesh. Then she told me to put the wallet down. My fingers just opened, and I threw it away from me. I was scared, but as soon as I got rid of the wallet the feeling left me.

"She put her arms around me and questioned me about what had happened. I told her I didn't feel it had happened yet, and I wanted to know what it was I had done. She said,

'It's all right, it's all right.' Then she kept questioning me about the room and the time. The only thing I could tell her was that it was cold outside and it was dark. It was cold in the room, too. She took that to mean it was early in the morning. The heat went off about midnight, and by three or four in the morning the rooms were quite chilly, especially in wintertime, which it was then.

"Grandmother had a man who was boarding with her, living in one of the rooms in her apartment, and he smoked cigarettes. Every time he woke up, he would light a cigarette. Sometimes he would go back to sleep without finishing it, and Grandmother had spoken to him about it many times. This time she got his cigarettes away from him before he went to bed, crushed them up, and threw them down the toilet. That didn't work because he had a cigar she didn't know about. Sometime during the night he lit it and placed it on the night table beside him. He also had to medicate himself, and he used to put alcohol on a piece of cotton and rub it on his leg. Well, he went to sleep with the cigar still going and that alcohol-soaked cotton lying right next to it on a paper doily. It all caught fire. When he woke up, the wallet was on fire and so were the sheets and pillow. He had just gotten his weekly paycheck, so he grabbed the wallet, got up, and ran out. He was badly burned and wound up in the hospital."

Tony continued to develop his gift and really didn't think too much about it. If you have psychic abilities, they aren't strange to you—just to others. He went through grammar school and high school, and then did college in three years. He wanted to join the navy but he was still under age and his mother wouldn't sign the papers. The only way he could get her to sign was by cutting school and getting her upset. After he cut classes on a postgraduate course for a sufficient time, his mother began to think that perhaps the navy could teach him some discipline.

When he was in boot camp, he met a fellow who was the only other psychic he'd met up to that time. The chap would talk about telekinesis, and Tony didn't know what it was. After boot camp, he married a girl named Jan. Then he was assigned to a psychological warfare unit in Korea. During an attack he was captured and placed in a prisoner-of-war camp for seven months; then Tony and some other prisoners managed to escape. After escaping, he was reassigned to duty in Japan. He had Jan flown over, and they had a great time together. Their son was born over there. Tony had to make short flights to Korea, and it was on one of those trips that he got word that Jan had been driving in the rain, had gone off the road over a cliff, and had been killed. He had only three months remaining on his enlistment, so he applied for an immediate discharge so he could take his infant son back to the United States and leave him with his grandmother.

Tony describes what happened: "I'll never forget that when I got ready to leave my grandmother said, 'I'll see you in four years.' She seemed to know something somehow, because I thought I would be back in a few months. I returned to Japan to clear up my affairs there. But I had a tremendous pull to the Mideast and Far East. I didn't know why, but there was a magnetic attraction to those areas. I really didn't know where I was going, just wandering at the time—but it proved to be just exactly what I wast supposed to do."

In Japan he visited Yokohama and Kamakura, then went to Taiwan, on to Hong Kong, the Philippines, and Indonesia, and wound up in Bombay.

It was while he was staying in an old British hotel that an incident occurred that changed his life dramatically. The temperature was between 120 and 125 degrees, outside and inside the room. He took a cold shower and stretched out on the bed completely nude. The large fan in the ceiling was going, but all it did was stir up the hot air. Out of the corner of his eye he noticed a slight movement and rolled over to see what it was. It was a deadly king cobra. The thought flashed through his mind that it was impossible for a snake to be up there in a third-story room. For some reason he didn't panic; rather, he said to it, "Hello, snake." With that, the snake, about two feet from him, struck him at the junction of his neck and shoulder.

Tony recounts what happened next: "Visualize a naked American, in a hotel lobby full of Europeans, taking ten stairs at a time, flying through the lobby, running out the front door of the hotel and down the street! I knew I had about eight minutes to live since that's how fast cobra venom works. The hospital was only a block and a half away, and I made it in twenty-two seconds flat! Of course I knew that the worst thing a snake-bitten person can do is run, but I would have died on the way if I'd walked. There were two Indian nurses on duty at the hospital, and I hoped they understood English. I pointed to the puncture marks and told them I'd been struck by a cobra. One of them did speak English, and she told me to lie down on the floor. They scurried around shouting in Indian. Two guys came running out—one of them stretched out on my legs, the other across my chest—and a doctor came charging in with a needle I swear was a foot long. I knew what he had to do, and I just hoped I could bear it. He stuck the damned needle in my stomach and I yelled with all my might. It felt like a sword had been run through me.

"I stayed in the hospital for a week and then went back to my room at the hotel. They had made a thorough search of the room and, sure enough, there were two king cobra snakes in there. The hotel couldn't understand how they had gotten up to the third floor of the building. The thing that bugged me was that they made me pay my hotel bill. I thought at least I should get a reduced rate for snakebite.

"That incident got me off my tour. While recovering from the bite, I spent my time, when it wasn't too hot, just wandering around looking at the shops, sightseeing. One day I walked through the shopping district. The blocks over there are like three or four of the blocks in this country. They were real long, then there would be a cross-street. I knew pretty well where the breaks were, so I didn't worry about getting lost. I got about halfway down the second block and saw a cross-street. I knew there hadn't been a cross-street there before, and I wondered if I was hallucinating because of the heat—you know how heat causes waves and mirages.

But it was there all right, and when I got to it I turned and went to the left; there was no one on the street.

"I walked about two hundred yards, and I got the weirdest feeling, as though somebody was watching me. I stopped and stood there for a moment, then thought I would go back the way I had come. When I started back, the street I had turned off was no longer there! I thought for sure the heat had gotten to me. Well, I thought that a street had to come into this long block somewhere, so I began walking and I walked about a mile. I never saw a person, not one; it was entirely deserted and there wasn't a sound.

"Finally I got to a cross-street and thought I would turn right and head back to the hotel. Just as I got to the intersection, an old man stepped out of a doorway; he had a cane that was as long as a staff, and he was absolutely naked. I wondered if he'd been bitten by a cobra—that's the first thing that crossed my mind. I just stopped and stood there. He approached me, never taking his eyes off me. When he got to me, I thought perhaps he wanted a handout. But he stopped in front of me, smiled, and said, 'Welcome, Anthony. I've been waiting for you!'

"The hair on my head stood straight up. It was so weird I turned and started walking to get away from him. I guess I walked about a hundred yards and then looked back. He was gone, and what is even more amazing, the cross-street also was gone. It was just a solid block of houses.

"I kept on walking another quarter of a mile, wondering who he was and how he had known my name. I came to another cross-street, and I turned left to get back to the hotel. Mind you, I still hadn't seen any people except the old man; everyone goes indoors for about five or six hours in the extreme heat of the day. I was the only one moving about. Just as I turned onto that cross-street, I *knew* I would see the old man again and my hair began standing up again. There he was. Again he smiled and said, 'Welcome Anthony. I've been waiting for you.'

"I was so shook that I got angry and said, 'Who the hell

are you?' He said, 'I'm your guru.' Then I said, 'You're my what?' He said, 'I'm your guru, your teacher.'

"I asked him what he was going to teach me. He replied, 'I'm going to teach you of yourself.' I told him I knew myself quite well, I'd been myself for over twenty-three years.

"I was really scared: A naked stranger comes up to you and says he's been waiting for you and he wants to teach you —what do you do, what do you think? He put his hand out and said, 'Come with me.' I asked him where, and he said, 'To my home. I will teach you.' I said, 'You want to bet?' I wasn't going anywhere with this old guy.

"He didn't make any other move toward me, but we kept talking. I asked, 'How long will it take?' He answered that it would take as long as it took.

"I finally decided that maybe he wasn't dangerous. He put his hand out again, and when I touched it a tremendous peace came over me. It seemed I had nothing else to say, nothing else to think. I went with him for about another mile and we turned into a building and went up to the second floor, where he lived. I moved my things out of the hotel and stayed with him for exactly ninety days.

"He taught me the basic teachings of Lao-tse—the philosophy of self, how to experience. My concentration exercises had begun with my grandmother, and he extended those to include deeper meditation, the blocking out of everything except what he told me to meditate on. The inner knowledge is tremendous when you get to the place where you can tap it. I learned to go within myself in a manner I'd never known before.

"At the end of the ninety days he told me my time with him was up and I was to leave. I had grown to love the old man, and when he told me I was to leave him the tears welled up in my eyes. I didn't want to go, but there was no way I could stay with him; that phase was over, and he told me my studies had to continue.

"I asked him where I would be going, and he said, 'You will go to Laos, and then to the village of Phu Lai. From there you will be taken to the Tsai Mei Lamasery on Phu Lai Leng mountain.'

"So I bought an airplane ticket and flew to Laos, then went by horseback all the way to Phu Lai and made contact with the caravan from the lamasery. We left for the lamasery on a Sunday morning. When I told the caravan master where I wanted to go, he said, 'Yes, I know. I am to take you there!' Everyone seemed to know about me and where I was going, and I didn't know anything about any of them. Actually, there was no fear, but there was anxiety and anticipation. I felt I had to do what I was doing because that was the way it was supposed to be. I did wonder if I was to stay in a lamasery for the rest of my life, and I thought, 'What a waste.'

"It was two hundred miles from the village to the lamasery. I didn't ride—I walked the whole way, and I wasn't tired at all. The weather wasn't hot, but it was humid. The country was a wild jungle, but it was beautiful.

"We finally got to the lamasery and went into a great big courtyard. The caravan dispersed and I just sat on my three pieces of luggage waiting for someone to come and say or do something. I tried to speak to a couple of people, but they completely ignored me. The lamasery is built on successive landings up the mountain, like different levels. I went up the first landing, looking for someone I could talk to. I was getting hungry. I walked down a corridor and finally saw a door at the end of it. I *knew* that was the door I had to go through.

"When I opened the door, there was an old man sitting in the squatting position with his legs under him, talking to two other lamas. I quietly closed the door, took my shoes off, and went over and sat down in the corner and just waited for about forty minutes. The two younger lamas finally got up and walked out. The old man then took the meditating position, the lotus position, with his eyes closed and his arms outstretched, palms up. I studied him for quite some time, and nothing happened. He just sat. Finally I got up and began slowly walking up to him. I guess I got to within a few feet and he hadn't moved, and then he opened one eye and rolled it at me. That flipped me. I began to laugh as though I had lost my mind. It was the funniest thing I'd ever seen. This old guy in the lotus position opening one eye to peer at me. He began to smile and then to laugh, too. I felt like a little kid getting caught in the act of doing something naughty. He knew what he was doing. It was a release for me, and any anxiety or fear I had was dispelled.

"Finally he said, 'Welcome, Anthony. I've been waiting for you.' There it was again! I said, 'Everybody is waiting for me but I don't know where I'm going or why I'm here.'

"The old man spoke English with a British accent. He was a very old man, and he looked it. About two months later I asked him how old he was and he said, 'One hundred and fifty seven.' I didn't know whether or not to believe him, but it wasn't that important.

"He clapped his hands; some other lamas came in with food and we had a good meal. He asked me about my other teacher and I told him. After lunch, he said he wanted to show me something. We went out of the room and down that corridor. The walls of the lamasery were very high, carved right out of the mountain. As we were walking down another corridor, I saw a huge mural about twenty feet high and sixty-five feet long, painted right on the mountain wall. It depicted all the centuries the lamasery had been there—about two thousand years. In each century the people in the mural were dressed the way they dressed at that time. I had gotten to the fourth century painting when suddenly I stopped; my hair went up and I had ice in my veins!

There was the painting of a young man—it was like looking into a mirror; it was my own reflection. His eyes were slanted a bit, his skin was neither yellow nor white, he was dressed in a toga-type garment, his hair was in bangs across his forehead, and he was holding a large scroll in his hands.

"The master asked me what the matter was. When I could find my tongue, I told him the young man in the painting was me. I just knew it. He didn't seem surprised; he just smiled and said, 'That is you in the fourth century.' The only thing I could stammer out was 'What about the scroll I was holding?' He told me I had been a scribe then, in the lamasery, had written the scroll over many years—and, after hiding it, had died in my sleep.

"He now wanted me to tell him or show him where the scroll was.

"The fourth century? Show them where the scroll was? I asked him how I was supposed to know, and so he explained. This was the first time I had ever really heard about reincarnation. I'd heard it mentioned before but hadn't paid any attention to it. He told me I was now the same age I had been in the fourth century when I wrote the scroll—just twenty-four. He told me that during that period there had been many wars going on. The troops had gotten very careless in their pillage and destruction; they were destroying the temples, but not the lamaseries. The temples contained all the written proofs, the teachings handed down from generation to generation. I had taken it upon myself to collect all the bits and pieces of information from other writings and had written them on the scroll. I wanted to protect it and so I had hidden it. But I died before I could reveal where I had hidden it.

"I asked him how he knew all this, and he showed me the record. It read just as I've told you, even to some Oriental medium having discovered where I was in the United States, and then in the navy and in Japan. And I had been mentally sent the messages that drew me to Bombay to meet my first guru, who then sent me on to Laos to the lamasery where I was at that very moment. The old man turned to me and said, 'Anthony, can you tell us what you did with the scroll?'

"That really threw me for a loop. I said, 'I don't even remember writing it.'

"Then he did a strange thing. He told me to look at the eyes of the young man in the mural—not to look at *his* eyes but to look at *my own* eyes in the painting, to concentrate on them. I concentrated on those eyes, and in just a few moments I was transported back to the fourth century. I was that young man again. My name then was Chien Le Tsien. I had come from a very poor family, and they had dedicated me to the temple and then to the lamasery. I relived my whole life in the fourth century, and the amazing part of it is that I still remember the details today. I remembered being born, growing up, my mother taking me with her into the fields. I remembered writing the scroll—I saw myself write it, then hide it, and then die.

"When I finally shook off the feeling of going back, my master was just standing and waiting, and he asked me again what I had done with the scroll. And this time I *knew* where it was.

"This whole recollection couldn't have taken more than a few minutes. I know it sounds unbelievable, but that's how it happened. The interesting thing is that I used the first-person singular when I answered him. I said that, when *I* had finished the scroll, *I* had put it under a slab in my cell, by the door. I remembered having to scoop the dirt out when I lifted that slab of rock up, to make a place for the scroll. *I* put it in there, replaced the slab, and covered the slab over with dirt.

"He got excited and clapped his hands. Three other lamas came running up, and he said something to them. They ran away and got some lanterns and tools; then we all went up another two levels and down a hallway until we came to a certain door; they had to jimmy it open. When we got inside the room, it smelled very musty. We had to step up to get inside because of the dirt on the floor. It was tamped down hard. They began to pick at the dirt. When they'd gotten down about eighteen inches, they hit rock. They cleared out a big area right where I had told them, by the door, where I'd seen myself bury the scroll. Then they used feathers to brush away the dust—and there was the outline of a slab. They worked at it for quite a while, very carefully, and then gently lifted the slab and then I almost went through the ceiling.

"The scroll was there! There was complete silence as we all stood and looked at it. It had been in that crypt from the fourth century—sixteen hundred years.

"All the hair on my body stood up again. I was covered with goose bumps. I just stood there looking from the scroll to the master, not knowing what to do. He said, 'Anthony, since you wrote the scroll for us, I think it is only fitting that you present it to the temple; I think it only right that you reach in the crypt and hand the scroll to me now.'

"I got down on all fours, reached in, took the scroll by one of the handles, and very carefully dragged it out. When I reached over with my other hand to grasp the other handle, a feeling almost like an electric shock ran up my arms and I felt a tingling throughout my body. And I felt very old. I do psychometry, and naturally I would get the predominant feeling. Then, too, I had been the last person to handle the scroll, even though it had been sixteen hundred years earlier.

"I stood up to hand the master the scroll, and he bowed very low before he touched it. I thought his head would touch the ground. Then he straightened up, took the scroll from my hands, and practically ran out of the cell.

"A month later the master explained my part in the presentation ceremony. Interestingly, when we set out for the temple I knew the steps and the turns—it was not strange to me. At the ceremony in the temple I knew I had been there before, as well. It was a very simple ceremony; there were only seven people present, including myself, but I knew literally a mass of people was observing. I found out later that there were forty-two hundred people at the lamasery. That will give you an idea of the vast size of the place, and yet you rarely saw more than a dozen people at any one time.

"The reincarnation idea kept bothering me. I kept trying to find ways to check it out. Finally I thought of checking the penmanship; maybe I had brought that back with me. The scroll was written in ancient Sanskrit, which apparently I didn't remember, so I had to have someone translate it for me and I wrote the same words in English. I wrote out a whole paragraph that had been translated from the scroll and then compared it with the handwriting on the scroll. It didn't look like that at all. But then the master told me to use the reflecting metal, meaning a mirror. (They used polished metal for mirrors.) When I placed the writing in the scroll and mine together and read mine in the mirror, backward, they were identical! The slanting of the letters, the endings of the letters, the curves of the e's, the shank and downward slash of the l's, even some of the numbers I had written—they all were identical to the same characters in the Sanskrit. There is no doubt in my mind that they absolutely matched, but in reverse. Now reincarnation makes sense to me; I don't know why it should, but it does."

Tony remained in the lamasery from 1952 to 1956. Finally the master called him in and told him that his learning had come to an end and he was now ready to reenter the world as a teacher. As Tony said, he really didn't want to go back *out there;* he even offered the master money if he could remain in the lamasery. But it wasn't to be, and the day came when he made the trip back to the village, then on to Bombay. An airplane carried him back to the United States. There had been no indication what his job as a teacher was to be, so he got a job in Glendale, California.

Tony had other astounding experiences while he was in the lamasery, enough to fill a whole book. Another memory he has had since that time is of the 1850s and the Civil War, when Tony Benik lived as the physical entity known as Lieutenant Jedidiah Alexander of the Confederate army.

Tony recounts the story.

"A few years ago I had an Akashic Record reading done by a psychic. When she was in full trance, she told me I had lived in the South in my past life and had fought in the Confederate army. This made sense to me because I've always had a deep feeling for the South; I love it, I love the rebel flag, the old mansions. I have a very strong relationship with the South, although I've never wanted to live there in this life. She told me I had been born in St. Petersburg, Florida, on March 11, 1844, that I had been married and had two children, both girls, and that I'd been killed by a sniper's bullet at the battle of Gettysburg in July of 1863.

"I thought, 'Gee, what an unromantic way of going,' I was nineteen years old when I was killed in that life. Then she told me that my history remains, which meant to me that somewhere there were records I could check out. She said my name had been Jedidiah Alexander. I asked her how I could get definite proof of all this.

"She said, 'Proof will be given to you personally, directly, within two weeks. You will receive the rifle you used while you were a soldier in the Confederate army.'

"I asked her how I could identify the rifle. It will be a cap-and-ball rifle, a short rifle. It will have the emblem of the eagle holding the arrows. It will have the date 1855 and Harpers Ferry stamped on it.'

"I thought that all the guns of that period would be about the same, made for the Confederate army, so I asked her if there would be anything different about it that I could recognize. Her reply was, 'The stock of the rifle was handcarved by you, and the pattern on the stock is elongated checks.'

"Exactly nine days later I received a long package from my aunt. She had cleaned out her garage and found two rifles, very old, she thought. Since I'd been in the service, she figured I might want them because they were unique; she didn't know how they had landed in her garage. One was a long cap-and-ball rifle; the other was a short cap-and-ball rifle with the emblem of the eagle holding the arrows on it. That short one had an inscription stamped on the metal: Harpers Ferry, 1855. The stock was handcarved, with elongated checks.

"When I held that smaller rifle, I picked up the sound of many men around me, as if I were in a camp. I couldn't pick out any particular voice; it was just a medley of sound, of people talking.

"I thought that, since my history remained, it would be in the archives in St. Augustine, Florida. When I went on vacation, I made a point to go to St. Augustine to check those archives. I told the girl at the desk in the Hall of Records what I was looking for: anything about a Jedidiah Alexander. She got out out a tintype of a young man with a woman and two little girls standing next to him. The name at the bottom of the tintype was the Jedidiah Alexander family!

"The only thing I recognized about me were the eyes: They spoke volumes to me; it was me. I didn't recognize the woman in the tintype or the two girls who had been my daughters. There was a letter I had written, but the penmanship was entirely different. All I could think of when I read those lines was, 'What lousy handwriting.' Also, there was a bullet pouch and a comb that had belonged to my wife. This proved to me that a Jedidiah Alexander had existed.

"Those are the only two lifetimes that prove to me that I existed previously on this planet. They've been checked out. If some Akashic reader tells me I have lived another life, I want proof of it before I'll believe it. Those two lifetimes checked out."

A friend of Tony's took a world tour a few years ago and visited the lamasery Tony had talked about. He saw the mural and agreed with Tony that it certainly did look like him. He also saw the scroll and the cell and crypt where it had been unearthed. The former head lama is now deceased, replaced by a lama who knows the whole story and has verified it.

When Tony left the Tsai Mei lamasery on October 1, 1956, the master gave him a sealed envelope and told him not to open it until April 1, 1970—some fourteen years later. Tony placed the envelope in a safe deposit box and did open it in April 1970. It contains, among other things, the following prophecies:

1. The nation under the Star of David shall cease to exist as a nation.

2. Great geographical changes will unfold throughout the planet.

3. The nation symbolized by the Great Eagle shall suffer internal strife, much of which will be recorded in history as the Dark Upheaval. Its people will be confused but patient with its cubs. A spiritual truth will come forth and make the Great Eagle truly great above all nations. Its power, influence, and love of spiritual freedom will bring many nations into its sphere of greatness. (Tony interprets the Great Eagle as the United States and its cubs as the "now" generation.)

4. Mankind will come very close to self-extermination by toxins. This is caused by man and can be corrected by man—*if* he so desires. If he does not make corrections, the law of nature will prevail.

5. The spiritual unity of all religions will be manifested.

6. Man shall discover his true heritage, and his greatness will unfold before his eyes, and he shall see and comprehend all wisdom of the ages. The Prince of Peace and Love shall rule forevermore.

7. The nation symbolized by the Maple Leaf (interpreted as Canada) and the nation symbolized by the Great Eagle (United States) shall join with each other in unity as one nation.

8. The signal of the beginning of these times shall be when the land of the many elephants shall join itself to other nations in war against the flag of scarlet. (Tony ploughed through many books that might refer to a nation as the land of the many elephants. In seven out of ten books Cambodia was listed as the land of many elephants. The flag of scarlet is the flag of communism, not of a particular Communist country.)

Then there followed three predictions indicating events in a time span covering the next fifty years:

1. A sign shall come from the western sky announcing the beginning of the end of all wars, forever.

2. The stone cat of the desert shall reveal its standing legs and lost knowledge and wisdom shall come forth from them. The first to unlock the ancient doors shall be three men, each from a nation of love and peace, and each of a different race.

3. The arrow of Aman-esh-nah shall pierce the sky and open it wide—the second sign that all peace shall be upon us. (Aman-esh-nah, in Laotian or lama lore, is a great messenger of God, not unlike the Angel Gabriel who split open the sky for the sign of Jesus when the constellations lined up and became known as the Star of Bethlehem.)

What has Tony done with himself since he was twenty-three and was led into the truly remarkable situations that gave him this phenomenal knowledge? He is not one of the occult buffs who run from psychic to psychic or astrologer to astrologer deluding himself or others with extravagant tales just to make himself a center of attention.

1. He has correctly read an individual's Akashic Record, and it has proven out to the individual's satisfaction.

2. As a clairaudient he has brought direct messages from those on the other side—friends, relatives, and acquaintances of those seeking word and evidence of continuing life.

3. He has clairvoyantly perceived objects or happenings that are not present to the normal senses. He has the ability of keen perception and great insight into those who come to him for readings.

4. He is a psychometrist who can hold and correctly read the history of objects belonging to or used by other persons.

About five years ago Tony was ordained and became Reverend Anthony Benik, Universal Christ Church. His mission is to help people in every manner he can, particularly spiritually. He is endowed with psychic abilities that have been developed over a long period of study and application. And he uses them.

11

Pictures in My Eyes

"The wagon wheel came down the hill and almost killed me. I was there."

That the girl saying those words was only three years old wasn't so remarkable, but the fact that she wasn't talking about her father, or her grandfather, but of having *been* her great grandfather, was astounding.

She kept saying, "I'm Grandpa Henry, I'm Grandpa Henry." It took some memory dredging for Monica's grandfather to remember that incident in the life of his father, and he'd only heard of it from his family; his father did have a slight limp all his life from that accident, which happened when he was very young. The family members all swear they had never mentioned the incident after Monica's birth.

Monica, now all of eight, had seen herself as her great grandfather when the wagon wheel came down the hill and ran over him. Had she really been who she said she was at that time, or was she witnessing a replay of the memory tape of time in her own consciousness, on her own personal recorder? The memory was bright, as she showed deep immediate concern when she was seeing it and saying the words, "I was there, and I was hurt."

That accident occurred in the 1880s, but Monica also witnessed something that happened about 1920, when her still living grandfather was a small boy in Illinois. Monica told the family of his house burning and everything being destroyed. She saw herself there at the time, and because it was burning she was again crying. The grandfather certified the story in detail, much to his own consternation. Had Monica tapped the microfilm library of his subconscious, or had she really been there at the time of the fire? Is Monica the physical replica of a reincarnated soul? Her great grandfather?

Monica Doland was born on August 15, 1961, at 10:02 A.M. in San Jose, California. Dark-haired, brown eyes, the pussycat face of the lovely Leo—quick and expressive. Mrs. Lucy Doland, Monica's mother, said that Monica didn't breathe for eleven minutes after her difficult birth; she was a preemie and a twin, but her brother died shortly after birth.

Monica was born with a caul. Today's dictionary definition is kind in its delineation of the word. A caul is a membrane enveloping the fetus that sometimes covers the head of the child at its birth. Being born with a caul is considered of signal portent and portends the birth of a prodigy, a marvel, a psychic. Not too many years ago being born with a caul was considered the advent of a witch or a seer. Most times it was looked upon as evil; the child was carefully watched to see if and when the devil or other evil discarnate/excarnate would manifest itself. If the child showed a love of cats, those cats were thought to be its familiars, evil ones doing the bidding of the witch.

Monica has the memory of having been one particular person when she has been in the scenes she saw. Further questioning elicited the information that she does do out-of-body travel. She can move about out there at will, quickly, wherever she wants to go, but she is always alone and has never recognized anyone she might have met. In the initial stages of her astral projection she sees her own body lying on the bed or couch or wherever she has gone to sleep. Without prompting from me, she said that sometimes she felt as though something had hit her hard, in the stomach, to awaken her. That indicates that, while she was going out of body, some noise or disturbance snapped her astral body back into her physical self with a bang. Monica said that sometimes when she is coming back it's as if she is riding downhill on a sled, very fast, being pulled by a rope. That rope could be the silver cord that is considered to connect the astral body with the physical counterpart.

Monica began exhibiting her paranormal abilities when she was just over two years old. Her grandfather had been taken to the hospital for an operation on an injured thumb. The family, including Monica, spent the afternoon at the hospital, waiting outside to hear how the operation and treatment were progressing. Monica was very distressed over the accident to her grandpa. At dinner that night she was so upset she couldn't eat her food. Lucy, Monica's mother, was adamant, and it became a clash of wills. Monica kept repeating, "I don't want it. I won't eat it."

Lucy and her mother, Ginnie Courtland, went on with their own dinner. Suddenly Lucy said, "Look at that!" Monica was looking fixedly into her plate, without touching it in any manner, and the plate was revolving as though someone was physically doing it.

Lucy said, "It went around in a circle three times. I leaned over and picked it up, because sometimes a dish has water under it and it will do that, turn, but the bottom of the plate was dry. We didn't know what to think."

What Monica was doing, and what the others saw, was a demonstration of telekinesis, the movement of an object without any visible physical means. Monica, because of her distress, was obviously emitting a tremendous psychic force that was causing the plate to revolve.

It was at about that same time that Monica began telling the family she saw pictures in her eyes. She would ask, "Do you see the beautiful lights, Mother?" Lucy couldn't see any pictures or lights. One night Monica described a vision:

"Over in the corner of my room, Mother, there is a cross made of lots of lights. It's God's mother standing there. There is a lady."

All this frightened Mrs. Doland. She knew very little of psychic phenomena, and to have a child possessing such abilities can be harrowing. Lucy took Monica to the church and asked her if what she saw in the pictures in her eyes was like the sun coming through the stained glass windows, outlining the saints. Monica said it wasn't—it was more a shower of lights.

One of Monica's amazing statements came one day when her grandmother was going to the doctor: She told her grandmother, Ginnie, that what she had was *opthalmovascularity,* then described it as the collapsing of the blood vessel that carries blood to the optic nerve. That a word and description of such medical precision could come out of the mouth of a child of seven was a bit unusual. It knocked the family members right out of their chairs! They wrote the word down as best they could.

The next morning, when Mrs. Courtland went to the opthalmologist, he ran the tests and came up with the same word and the same diagnosis. I asked Mrs. Courtland if she told him about Monica's diagnosis, which she had. The doctor's reaction was a noncommittal "Uh, very interesting." Obviously, either he didn't believe it or a psychic phenomenon was out of his department.

The unverifiable scenes that Monica has seen and described are many. In one instance, while riding along in the car with her mother, she received the distinct vision of an airplane crashing and she became highly agitated. Another was of an auto accident and was so real Monica hid her head in her mother's lap; still another was of a boy striking another boy with a baseball bat and knocking him down and out.

A child endowed with psychic gifts will ultimately be found out by his or her peers, and children aren't known for their tolerance or understanding of the unusual any more than adults are. Monica has changed schools twice, both times to avoid the slings and arrows of outrageous ridicule as a spook, a nut. It's gotten to the point where she now hesitates to tell her mother all the events she sees in her mental pictures.

While she was still living in San Jose with her family, she dreamed "they" were taking a dead person out of the apartment right under the one occupied by her grandmother. When she awakened, she told Lucy of the dream and was afraid it might have been her grandmother she saw. Lucy didn't pay attention to her. The next morning Ginnie came over from Oakland for a visit and was told of the dream. They all had a good laugh, but Monica kept insisting somebody had died. Two days later the man living in the apartment below Mrs. Courtland was taken out, dead from an overdose of sleeping pills. His death had occurred, or was occurring at the time Monica saw it.

Monica's precognitive ability is quite high. Just as she was dropping off to sleep one night, she was seized with a bad headache and saw a woman friend of the family who lived down the street having something happen to her head. The headache was so severe Monica couldn't sleep, and she got up to tell her mother. In half an hour the headache was completely gone and she returned to bed. In the morning their next-door neighbor came in to tell them the woman friend down the street had had a stroke during the night and had been taken to the hospital.

Another night Monica picked up a scene of Grandmother Courtland coming down the stairs of her apartment through a cloud of smoke, as if the place were on fire. The next morning Mrs. Courtland called to say there had been a fire in one of the apartments in the building and the girl living in it was almost overcome by the smoke before she could get out and down the stairs. Monica saw it at the time of the occurrence. Being primarily concerned with her grandmother, Monica saw the figure coming through the smoke as Mrs. Courtland. It was a transference, but in the same apartment building.

Just prior to the birth of Monica's sister, Vickie, the members of the family were speculating on the expected child's sex, body length, and birth weight. Monica came up with "Girl, 18 inches long, a little over six pounds." (Monica was all of five and a half now.) She was right.

An interesting comment here could be that *if* Monica is her own great grandfather, she also has other extrasensory gifts and they are obviously tied very closely to her grandfather, father, and family, and to her very close friends. At a very young age she *remembered* having been her own great grandfather and an accident she'd had in that life. She has out-of-body experiences during which she *sees* things that are happening. She possesses precognition, has *seen* occurrences that haven't physically happened but ultimately do. And she demonstrated retrocognition in the case of having *seen* the house burning when her grandfather was a small boy. She has experienced telekinesis—the movement of objects in her presence without a visible force doing the moving. Monica exhibited clairvoyance when she *saw* her grandmother's optic problem; witnessed unverified scenes, such as the airplane crashing, an automobile accident, a boy striking another boy with a ball bat; developed a sick headache, *seeing* a woman friend of the family having something wrong with her head; visualized the scene of Grandmother Courtland coming down the smoky stairs of her apartment. She can be tested for psi phenomenon, but the reincarnative recollection must remain unresolved.

12

I Was Waiting to Be Born Again

"Yes, there I was, sitting on this fence, just waiting to be born into this body. I knew who I was. I was me, waiting to be born again. I don't know who I was in the former life, but I've often wondered. I have no recollection of that particular life, except, as I say, I was *me*, always me—and I was born into this body on a ranch in Las Cruces, New Mexico."

Yvonne, in this life, is an attractive, vivacious, auburn haired woman in her middle thirties. Currently, she is an executive with a public relations company in Hollywood.

"I was a girl, and I knew I would go into the body of the child that would be born in that ranchhouse, so I was waiting. I would walk around the place, sit on the fence, go into the house and see how things were coming along with my new mother.

"I picked my parents. I don't know *how* I picked them, but I knew I would become the baby my mother was carrying. It was just a question of time. So I waited around."

I was so astounded by what this woman was telling me, I asked her, "When was this dream? How old were you?"

"It wasn't a dream. It was just as real as I'm telling it to you. I had been in another body. Now I was going into a new one, to experience another life cycle. This time I would be called Yvonne ———. I knew what my name would be. I had been in the house enough times to hear my new parents talk over the name they would give me if I was a girl. When they were picking the name, I tried to send them the name Yvonne, and they must have gotten it. If I had been a boy, they would have called me Robert. I remember how I laughed because they didn't know which sex I would be. I knew.

"While I was sitting around waiting to be born, I had on some kind of a loose robelike garment, not heavy or light, just a garment. It was gray-white in color. I wasn't aware of any heat or cold, but I knew when it was day or night. I used to love to watch the sun come up, the new day dawn while I sat on the fence. After I got born and was old enough to run around, I remembered the fence and would sit on it and know why I was doing it. As far as getting hungry, I knew I wasn't in a physical body and food wasn't important to me. I also knew that, when I was born into this body, I could then be hungry and get cold, and all the things you experience on this earthly plane.

"I don't know how long I had been out of the other body before I was born into this life. I just knew I had been in another life cycle and now was entering a new one. It just seemed as natural as breathing. There wasn't anyone else around, any other spirit or spirits, when I was waiting to be born. Just me, hanging around the ranch. I would have known if there were other out-of-body spirits around. I also knew I couldn't be seen by my new folks or any of the people who came to visit during the time my mother was carrying me. They were solid; I wasn't. I knew I could talk to them but they couldn't hear me.

"When I was about to be born, I knew it was getting close and I knew the conditon of my new body, somehow. Actually I wasn't born in that house. My father became real nervous and talked my mother into going down into the valley to her folks, to my grandparents' place—another ranch. My dad hitched up the team, put my mother in the wagon, and off they went. I went along, too. Not in the wagon, but staying above it, around it.

"All I remember of the actual birth was that I was outside my grandparents' house, just sort of hanging around. Then everything seemed to grow hazy and dim—and then suddenly it was just as though the lights went out. That was the end—and the beginning, I guess.

"The memory must have come to me when I was about three or four. It was very strong, and I remember I would toddle around the ranch and go to the places, like the fence, the barn, where I had gone before I came into this body. It's something you just know. And another thing—when I was about three or four I would see other spirits—I guess you would call them that—and we would actually have conversations. My parents would sometimes ask me whom I was talking to, and I told them 'my friends.' They just thought I was having childish imaginings, but those other spirits were there. I knew they were spirits and they were real to me. When I got older, either my friends over there came around less often or I lost the ability to see them. Anyway, they finally left and I haven't seen anything like that since I was a little girl."

How did I meet Yvonne? My wife was having lunch in her favorite eatery one day and struck up a conversation with a young lady sitting nearby. When Florence told the girl about this book project, she said she had a friend who had memories of former lives. Yvonne turned out to be a commercial artist with a large company in Hollywood. I was truly impressed at the number of book covers she'd done.

After she'd finished the story of her birth into this life, she said, "There is one other incident I've had. I *saw* myself in another life. The only way I can describe it is to say I was flipping along under the telephone wires! It was as if I were using the energy from the wires. It seems I traveled along under those wires until I got to Texas. (I lived in California at the time this incident happened, about seventeen years ago.) I had been doing some study on out-of-body travels, and knew it was possible. I'd never done it before, but I knew it could be done. This study course had some exercises to help a person do astral projection, and I was fascinated by it. I had been trying exercises—staring at a candle flame, looking fixedly at myself in a mirror in a darkened room. I got so I could go out of body, but I couldn't seem to control the times I went or where I went. It would just happen all of a sudden.

"Anyway, on this trip to Texas I came to a stop, for some reason, and I found myself looking at an old adobe house. I went over to the house and looked in a small window. I knew that when I looked in that window I would see myself in a past life!

"Inside the house there was a very old woman. It was me, and I knew it. As I watched, I wondered what I had looked like when I was younger, and right away that other me seemed to grow younger until I was about forty years old. I had a pack on my back and realized that I had a baby, carrying it as an Indian carries a papoose. I thought to myself, 'Oh, for heaven's sake, do I always have to have children?' You see, I was having quite a struggle taking care of my son in this life. I was trying to work and find someone to take care of him. It was rough.

"I watched myself very quickly go from that woman in her seventies back thirty years to a woman in her forties with a child. I was definitely a frontier woman in that life, and I carried my child in a pack on my back. I wanted to see what this place looked like, so I started to walk around and a young girl ran up to me.

"When she did, I knew I was astrally projected and I was no longer experiencing the memory of the woman in the adobe house. This girl seemed to have two boy friends, and she was asking my advice about which one she should choose. The two boys were standing nearby. When she began talking to me about them, one of them ran up and grabbed her by the hand and led her away.

" 'So,' I thought, 'now I'm going to go somewhere else! I'd

seen that lifetime, a little bit of it, and since I had the chance I might as well see some more. I made a huge leap, to jump up into the air and fly, and suddenly I was right back in this body, waking up.

"I found out, when I was doing out-of-body travel, that whenever I decided to do something on my own I would end up right back in this body. When I did projection, I just had to let *it* take me where *it* wanted to, not where I wanted to go. When you're doing astral projection, if you think about your own body you go right back to it. People have told me they are afraid to practice astral projection since they might not be able to get back, but I've found, and heard from others, that all you have to do is think about coming back and you're back in your body—sometimes with a real thump.

"As far as time goes, I don't really know how long that incident in Texas lasted. I do know that it was the first time, and it was the most exhilarating thing that had ever happened to me. Such freedom! But I've also found that it can be dangerous. When you exteriorize, it isn't good to remain earth-bound. Astral projection should be used to visit other, higher planes, not stay on the dense plane connected with Earth. That is the lowest form of projection—the plane just beyond this physical one. Everything that is in the physical plane is also in the lower astral plane. I was experiencing what was in that lower plane—all the pictures of everything we've done. It's all there, and we can look at them. They are the Akashic records, the records of your lives, and you can read them in astral travel.

"Another experience I had was also out of my body. I went out through my head this time, which is quite natural once you know the various methods of getting out of your body. When I was finally out, I said 'I want to go where I can learn the most.' The next thing I knew, I was going down, into a big black crevice. It got darker and darker, and that really frightened me. I said, 'No, no, I want to go up,' and I started floating up. In this absolutely black wall there was a light, like a window or a door. I went through it and found myself in what seemed to be an attic. There were a whole bunch of children there, and they all ran up to me crying, 'Momma, Momma.' Here I was again, a mother! I said, 'I'm not your mother.'

"Then I walked down what seemed to be four or five steps to a room where there was an old man sitting in a rocking chair. I didn't think he could see me. I tripped over a little rug on the floor. He looked up at me and said, 'The children are going to get blamed for that.' One of the children had followed me down the steps into this room. I turned to him and said, 'Straighten that up, will you please,' and he did. I looked from that room into another room where a woman was scolding another woman who looked like a maid. I said to myself, 'I ought to tweak her nose,' because I figured she couldn't see me.

"You see, what I didn't realize at the time was that this was another past life of mine I was seeing. Those kids were all mine, the old man was probably some relative I had taken care of, and the woman scolding the maid so viciously was me. One of those kids took me by the hand and I started toward the door. As I walked through the door, back into the light—bang, I was back in my own body, right here in Hollywood.

"In that life I had seen myself as the mother of a whole flock of kids; I had a maid, and I was a very carping woman. In that sequence I was dressed in one of those old-fashioned long dresses, hem to the ground and high around the neck with a lace collar.

"The interesting thing in all of these recollections was that I never for a moment forgot that I was and am Yvonne having those experiences. Everything in each incident was just as clear as a bell; there was nothing dreamlike about any of them. Usually in my dreams I am watching someone else do something, but when I go out of body I am the one doing the things, going to all those places.

"There is one other recollection I have. I don't remember how I got there, although I had been meditating on out-of-body travel, but I don't remember leaving my body this time. I was in a forest and I was talking to Jim Bowie. You know, the guy with the knives, back in the old days, down south. Jim was teasing me about my hair; he was going to cut my long hair off so the other guys wouldn't give me so much attention.

"There were some other men around—his friends, I guess—and they were all laughing at him about some product he was promoting at the time. When I came out of that experience, every time I thought about it I would wonder: What in the world was that product they were kidding him about? About six months later there was a television series on called 'Jim Bowie.' It came on at five-thirty or six o'clock every evening. I would come home from work and turn on that show while I was getting dinner for my son and me. One night while I was getting out of my car the thought suddenly struck me—chokeberries. I thought that was odd—chokeberries. I'd never really heard of that kind of berries. I went into the house and turned on the television to the 'Jim Bowie' show. I was in the kitchen, and every so often I would walk out into the living room and look at the show, mostly hearing it rather than seeing it. And once I walked in for my little moment of watching and Jim Bowie was saying, 'As soon as I wash the chokeberries off my face, I'll be with you.' That was what those fellows had been teasing Bowie about when I visited that former life of mine! It was down around New Orleans and Jim was in business there; this time he was trying to get people interested in eating chokeberries.

"At the time I had the recollection of being in the life with Jim Bowie, the television series wasn't on the air. It came later. The subconscious is always coming up with little tidbits of information about things we think we never knew or heard of. Sometimes we receive telepathic messages from someone else and wonder what in the world is going on. It happens all the time, and at times we get glimpses of events in a former life."

13

Reincarnation and Continuing Life

Throughout history women have been out in front when it comes to delving into the paranormal. That sterling character Pythagoras, erudite philosopher and unequaled mathematician, fell into the male chauvinist role and espoused the idea that there was a *good* principle that created order, light, and *man*, and an evil principle that created chaos, darkness, and *woman*! When the male becomes particularly insecure, he always accuses the female of being different, being on another wavelength.

Many bona fide occult practitioners have to protect themselves from the courts and possibly jail by obtaining the title of reverend, by whatever means. (This is particularly true in California, where occultism is prohibited by law unless it is a religion.) A type of spurious credential can be obtained from a proffering "institute" for about forty-five dollars.

When I first heard of Reverend Jean and the type of work she did, my reaction was: "Here we go, again." I was delighted to find I was wrong. She is an authentic minister, an honorable woman possessed of psychic gifts who offers honest counsel drawn from great insight into humanity. I was told she had an interesting view of reincarnation, and also did out-of-body travel to other, higher planes of existence. Her main concern is with people who are in search of increased spiritual understanding in a world that is seemingly going madder by the generation.

I set up an appointment with her in her home in Hollywood. When we got down to her concept of reincarnation, it was so different from anything I knew that at first I felt it couldn't be reported here. However, after listening to the tape a few times, I felt it had to be included.

Here is Reverend Jean, all of five-foot-two, with her graying brown hair, her placid exterior, and her direct, intense inner fire:

"Before I was taken to the halls of learning on the high planes, I rationalized all this just as most people do—that there is reincarnation, and anyone who didn't believe it was true must be wrong since I was right. I had the same arguments that everyone else has for it, such as why some children are smart and some are not, some are geniuses and some are little dodos. Of course there is a reason for some of these memories, or supposed memories, and many of what are called former lives are really disembodied spirits who are reliving their lives through Earth beings. The people who are being visited by the spirits don't know what is happening and think they are getting their own life experiences.

"You see, I work with many people, removing obsessions. Let me give you an example. I was in a market, here on Hollywood Boulevard. A woman had a very young child in a stroller. I looked at the little fellow as I passed by, and I felt I was looking at an aged man. I stopped and bent down and looked into his face, because I couldn't believe what I saw. That little infant looked right back at me with one of the most severe expressions, like a cranky or crabby old man. I began to concentrate on him, to see if I could pick up his vibrations, maybe find out what was going on.

Time-Tripping and Projection

"Do you know what? The grandfather had taken possession of that little boy!

"And the grandfather didn't like my vibration, I suppose. This angered me, so I said to him, 'What are you doing with that baby?' And he said, 'You mind your own damned business; I'm reincarnating, and this is my grandson.'

"The baby wasn't old enough to walk yet. I would say he was about eight or nine months old. But his grandfather, who was in the other dimension in spirit, said that to me when I asked him what he was doing with the baby. The grandfather was speaking to me in my mind. I tried to talk to him, to reason with him, to get him to let go of the child. Just then the grandmother came bustling up in a sort of irritated frame of mind. She grabbed the stroller and pushed it out of the market, so that was the end of that. Now that was a reincarnation for you; even the grandfather felt it.

"I had another instance of a woman who brought her eight-year-old daughter to me. She had suddenly lapsed into a very obstreperous type of behavior; no one could do anything with her. The teacher brought this to the mother's attention; and through someone who knew me the mother brought the girl to me because they couldn't control her. Pure and simple, she was after the boys—and she wasn't kidding! She was telling everyone she was going to have a baby, and the whole bit.

"The mother was terrified. She'd had the girl to psychiatrists. Nothing seemed to work, so she brought her to me. I saw that there was a woman obsessing her—a woman who had been a streetwalker, a prostitute.

"I had the little girl sit in a chair I call the magic chair, and I talked to the female who was obsessing her. I asked, 'What are you doing with this little girl? What's the big idea, invading her mind and body? Don't you know this is all wrong?' Well, she became very hostile—the streetwalker, you know—and she told me off in no uncertain terms. She said, 'It's my business what I'm doing. I'm not hurting her; I'm only reincarnating through her.'

"The girl and I had a number of sessions, and that woman

invading her and I had some long talks. We went round and round for a long time, until finally she was convinced that she might be hurting the girl's life just as her own life had been hurt when she was young. When she realized what she was doing was bad, she just left.

"The girl sort of snapped out of a dazed condition. It was just as though she was coming out of a spell or a partial trance. She looked around and asked, 'Mommy, where are we?' That's how thoroughly taken over by that female she had been.

"Speaking medically, that would be called a case of possession, but those people on the other side think they are reincarnating.

"I have a staff of assistants who work with me on the invisible side of life, the other side. They are missionaries, and each is an expert in a specific line that may need to help someone in trouble. They work with humanity, for humanity, for release and uplifting, for education and the progress of mankind.

"They are my instructors; they are my teachers and directors. There is also a band of missionaries and doctors and experts in their own fields who are interested in mankind. They use me as the battery. Why don't they use somebody on that side of life? They have to use someone in the physical body as the battery between the two worlds."

This was all fascinating, but I had not heard any personal memories or dreams of reincarnation, so I asked, "Have you ever realized or thought that you were the reincarnation of someone else?"

"I have thought about this. I gave it quite a bit of thought, and naturally, as I said in the beginning, I did think just like everybody else. But no, I've never reincarnated—not as you are talking about it, coming back into physical life after having lived before.

"You know, everybody thinks they were something a little better, a little higher than they are now. In my own opinion, if reincarnation was a fact, that would be retrogression—not progression from life to life. I believe that those on the other side come into an Earth person and make that person feel as if he is reincarnated.

"Here's a story that will interest you. I had a woman tell me she had had many reincarnations. And, in this life she thought she was the reincarnation of the Virgin Mary. This irked me. I've heard all this before, so I said to her, 'So you're the Virgin Mary. I always wondered what had become of her. We hear so much about her son, once in a while about her husband, but what about dear Mary?'

"She looked at me, rather startled, and I said, 'How come you, of this high estate, have become so much less than you were then? Explain this to me. I want to learn, I want to know.'

"She said, 'Well, I don't know. I just fell from grace.' And she looked so sad. I told her that if she was the Virgin Mary then at one time she had a brilliant vibration, a very developed soul light—and where was her soul-light now? And I asked her, 'And what's with your vibration? Your aura? Your aura is terrible, and your vibration is even worse.' In that same year I met seven women who thought they were the Virgin Mary!

"The way reincarnation is taught to me in the halls of learning on the other side of life is entirely different. Of course I asked my teachers about it, and I've been taken to the lectures that are conducted by master souls on the high plane. Now I'm not talking about the astral area. You hear so much about astral travel. People say, 'Oh, I've been in the astral plane; I do astral travel.' I get annoyed with that too. I ask them why they remain in the astral, why they don't go beyond it. After all we all enjoy slumming once in a while, but we wouldn't want to live there, would we? Some people are satisfied to enter the astral world as heaven, but it isn't. It's just part of the physical world, the material world. The astral level has the vibration of the earth world, the dwelling of the disembodied entities who have not advanced beyond it.

"To get back to reincarnation, it has been shown to me that the best education is visual, and on the other side it is also by transmission of thought—a blending of thought vibrations. I attended a lecture conducted by one of the masters, and there were some very ancient beings sitting there. I was taken there by my master. I couldn't go there on my own; I haven't evolved that far, you understand; I don't want to create the wrong impression. The room in which we had the lecture was in a U-shape, and all the chairs were in the same U-shape. I have never seen anything so white as that place was, everything in there. A white radiance is the only way I can describe it. There wasn't a sound at any time, yet I knew every word that was being said by thought transmission.

"They taught that, once conception takes place, this is the last descent of the life germ into the Earth's atmosphere, because it picks up a personality, picks up a body. Up to that time it can dip down into the Earth's vibration and be carried in the bloodstream of different people. This happens many, many times, and for long periods of time.

"While it is being carried in the bloodstream or the vesicles, it is possible for the germ to retain in memory—genetic memory—its experience with someone in their body. People misinterpret this as having been a reincarnation, which in a sense it is. Medical science has proved conclusively that every time a conception takes place there are millions—hundreds of millions—of germs of life that don't connect with the ovum. There is only one that connects, or two, sometimes three or four, seldom five. The question is: Since life is indestructible, where do they go, those other millions of germs? What becomes of the germs that have been ejected by the male? They are drawn back into the cosmic ocean of life to once again gyrate and spin around and once again, by the laws of attraction, be drawn into another individual and remain there for a certain length of time, until another period of ejection and expulsion comes. This could happen to one germ of life many times, and if the germ does connect, that could be considered an incarnation, or reincarnation, depending on the belief of the person you are talking to.

"The germs of life go through a process of development, almost like a universal education. They are not all learning at the same rate of speed, any more than our children here in school. But when a germ has reached this point of ripening, then through the law of attraction, the law of love, it is drawn into this Earth sphere, physically, and given expression by coming into Earth life.

"You are who you are because you have a face—you have established an identity. If you didn't have a face, no one would know who you were! That is what the word 'persona' means—face, person, individual. It's simple when you stop to think about it. I've been asked just *why* we really are what we are, why we are actually in being. I can't answer that, except to say, 'God's will be done'—and we are of God. Do you know the mind of God? Does anyone? My masters don't; they have an idea, but it's much like ours: 'There is something *higher,* something or someone *else.*' It is all spiritual."

14

Dreaming True

"I do what I call 'dreaming true,' have been doing it for many years, and I can project my astral or dream body during sleep when I want to, and go where I want to go. It was during one of those times that I first met the little girl who had been my daughter in a former life."

Martin and I were sitting and talking in his living room in Seattle, Washington. I judged him to be in his middle thirties, slightly balding, blue eyes, of medium height. I asked him to explain what "dreaming true" was.

"Well, the best way to explain it is that when I lie down to sleep I consciously picture in my mind what I would like to dream of—a place, a person. When I get to the point where I'm slipping into sleep, I transfer myself into the dream scene I have created. The more you do it the more easily and the better it works.

"I've been doing this for about five years. I stumbled on it by accident the first time. I had been studying pretty hard for some exams for a new job, and I was just about exhausted. I was really worried. I had gone to bed that night thinking how nice it would be if I could just somehow escape for a while. I began picturing a scene in my mind of the place I had lived in Montana when I was a kid. It was a small ranch; we ran about two hundred head of cattle and farmed about a hundred and fifty acres. A creek ran along the northern boundary of our property. I would go there when I was little, and that was my own secret getaway place. This time I pictured the scene, and just as I was falling asleep, I just kind of stepped into the picture—and there I was! I was actually back there in Montana, at the creek. At that time I didn't know anything about astral projection, or any of that kind of thing, but I did think I was dreaming and that it was great.

"I walked down to the creek, sat down, took off my shoes and socks, and put my feet into the water. It felt so good I took all my clothes off and jumped in, just as I had when I went there years ago. I felt the water; it was as cold as I remembered it. I stubbed my toe on a rock, and it hurt. I kept saying to myself, 'Boy, this is no dream.' That's how real it was. I finally got out and ran around the field for about five minutes to dry off.

"I've also found that, when you dream true, you enter into the picture just as you created it, and usually I don't go anywhere except right where I created the picture. But sometimes I have created a picture and when I step into it something has gone wrong because it isn't what I set up. That can get a little confusing at times. Once I wanted to visit some friends in Illinois and I wound up sitting in the dining room with some people I'd never seen before, watching them eat dinner."

What Martin had described so far is purely out-of-body travel during sleep and would have no place here except for the continuing phenomenon of the girl who had been his daughter.

"To someone who has never done this type of thing, it is unbelievable, I know. It even threw me at first, and I thought I was really hallucinating—until I began to check it out and found it was true. I'd never, up to that time, had much truck with reincarnation. Not that I didn't hope it was true, but I had never been convinced of it.

"In this current life I had a daughter named Kathy. She was a beautiful child, blonde and blue-eyed, and she did seem closer to me, or I was closer to her, than she and her mother were. She liked to go to sleep on my lap. When we went for a ride in the car, she would get in the back seat, on a mattress we had there flush with the top of the seat, and go to sleep with her head on my shoulder. We seemed to have quite a mental and emotional rapport. Sometimes her mother would be miffed because Kathy and I were so close, but I hear that in a lot of families the girl is closer to the father.

"Anyway, when she was just about four years old she came down with what the doctor diagnosed as a type of meningitis, a virus. They put her in the hospital and did everything possible, but they couldn't save her. Kathy would be going on eleven if she had lived. She died on October 21, the day before her fourth birthday. I was twenty-eight. I'm thirty-five now. This was almost seven years ago.

"I didn't begin dreaming true right away; that started about two years after Kathy died, and the first dream trip was the one to the ranch. That was so terrific that I began trying to do it all the time, and it wasn't until I learned to just picture one thing that it really began to work and I could step over into the dream I had created and take part.

"The first time I had a dream where I met with Kathy was about three years ago. I'd gotten to doing the dreaming thing quite a good deal, and I would tell my wife about it. She didn't dig it at all. I hadn't started dreaming about Kathy at that time, but about going to a lot of other places and seeing other people. Kathy's death had always weighed on my wife, and eventually we couldn't get along about anything and we got a divorce. One night I was getting ready to go to sleep and I thought of Kathy and wondered if I could dream up a scene where she would be present. I held onto the picture, of Kathy playing in the backyard as she used to—and just as I was slipping into sleep I stepped over into the scene. Although I had pictured Kathy in detail, when

Time-Tripping and Projection

I got into the dream picture there was a girl but she didn't look like Kathy. I thought, 'That's funny. Where did that girl come from?' So I asked her who she was.

"She told me her name was Kathy before, 'but now it's Marjorie.'

"I said, 'that was my daughter's name, Kathy.'

"Then she said, 'I am your daughter.'

" 'Do you know who I am?' I asked.

" 'You are my daddy.'

" 'What are you doing here?'

" 'I came to find you—I knew where you lived.'

" 'Where do you live?'

" 'I live on G——— Street.'

" 'But my daughter Kathy is dead. She's been dead a long time. Do you know what death is?'

" 'Yes, but I only died for a little while when I was Kathy—and now I am somebody else's daughter, but I am your daughter, too.'

" 'Why didn't you come before?'

" 'I did, but you didn't see me.'

" 'Did you come in the house?'

" 'No, I couldn't go in the house.'

" 'Why couldn't you?'

" 'I don't know.'

" 'I am having a dream now, and I am dreaming about you; that is why you are here.'

" 'I have dreams too, but they are real, and now I am here.'

"Well, we walked around the yard for a while, just as Kathy and I had done. Then she said, 'I have to go now; will you come out to see me if I come again?'

"I told her I sure would. I still thought I was dreaming and it was nice but it didn't mean anything—it was just a dream. I told her the next time she went to sleep she should come and see me, the next night, and I would go to sleep and come to see her, right there in the yard. She said she would, and then she turned and walked right up to the gate in the fence, reached up and opened it, and went out and closed it. Usually I go to bed about ten-thirty or eleven, and the moment Kathy was gone I awakened. I turned on the light and looked at the clock: It showed three-thirty, so I had been asleep about three and a half or four hours.

"That day I went to work in a daze. The dream had been so real, and I really didn't want to believe it was anything but a dream. I was afraid it might drive me bats if I kept it up. Yet I'd done a lot of this type of dreaming, and the other dreams were real, so why not this one? The whole thing was pretty confused in my mind."

The magnitude of what Martin had just told me had me confused, too. If it was true, then here was a case of "boomerang" reincarnation like nothing I'd ever heard or read. There were three verifiables at this point:

1. The address Kathy had given as her home, and it was there in Seattle, not a mile away.

2. That her name was Marjorie in this life.

3. That she would be the same child Martin saw in his dream.

Martin continued his story. "The next night I went to bed around nine-thirty, just to see if I could make a longer contact with Kathy—I mean Marjorie—again. I held the picture of the backyard in my mind, with Kathy being there, just as I had the night before. When I felt myself going into sleep, I stepped right over into the picture of the backyard. Kathy was there, still looking like Marjorie. She came running and threw her arms around me. I was so happy to see her I cried. This was unbelievable—Kathy was dead and I was having contact, physical contact with her through another physical body she said was hers in this life.

" 'What shall I call you? Kathy or Marjorie?'

" 'When I am with you, I am Kathy.'

" 'All right, Kathy. I'd like to ask you some questions.'

"She took my hand, and we walked over and sat down on the steps of the back porch. I had to find out more about her life before she died, when she died, and if she had any memories about what happened to her when she came back into this life as Marjorie.

" 'Kathy, you said you had died; do you know how, do you know what caused it?'

" 'I was very sick. The doctor came, but he couldn't do anything for me. He put me in the hospital. You were very sad, and so was Mother. You cried because I was so sick.'

" 'What happened in the hospital; do you remember anything then, or when you couldn't talk to us?'

" 'I could hear you. I could see you, too, but you couldn't hear me. The doctor came and took me away on a cart and did some things to me.'

" 'Do you know what causes death, Kathy, how it happens?'

" 'You just stop breathing, and then I guess you are dead.'

" 'Is that what happened to you?'

" 'When I couldn't breathe anymore, I went away. I went with my friends.'

" 'What friends? Who were they?'

" 'The boys and girls who came and talked to me while I was sick. They told me I would be all right when I could come with them, and then I went with them and I wasn't sick anymore.'

"I've done some reading on the subject of pre-and post-death occurrences, and I wanted to be very careful I found out whether they were true or not. You see, I'd never had what could be called psychic experiences, not the kind I've heard and read about people having. The closest thing has been this dreaming true, and then this happened.

" 'Kathy, just before you went with the doctor, do you remember seeing anyone in your room?'

" 'Yes. You and Mother and the doctor and a nurse. And the doctor called a man to come and get me; he had a cart he put me on.'

" 'What did the doctor do to you when he took you away?'

" 'He put me in a big room and they put some long needles in my neck and in my arms. Then the doctor said I was dead.'

" 'What happened then?'

" 'The doctor went back to the room you were in, and you and Mother cried real hard. I tried to tell you I was all right.

My friends told me you couldn't hear me. The doctor and the nurse cried, too.'

" 'How long have you been coming to see me, Kathy?'

" 'A long time, but you couldn't see me. And now you can.'

" 'Could I see you if I came to your house on G——— Street?'

" 'Yes.'

" 'Would you know me if I came to visit?'

" 'Yes.'

" 'Do your mother and father know that you were my daughter before you were their daughter?'

" 'I told them, but they just think I am making up stories. I told them my other daddy lived here, and I had lived with you before I came to live with them.'

" 'Kathy, let's play a game. I will come to your house to repair something, but you mustn't let them know who I am. We will play a game; I will just be the repairman, okay?'

" 'Okay. When will you come?'

" 'I don't know. When you hear that the repairman is coming, you'll know it's me. I'll try to do it in a few days.'

"We got up, and this time I walked her to the gate and opened it. She walked out, then she disappeared, or I went back into my body. The sequence was over and I woke up. I got right up and wrote it all down."

Martin managed to show up at Kathy's house on the pretext of being a public utilities representative making a repair. He met the parents.

"It wasn't any trouble, getting in. Kathy wasn't there immediately, she was playing outside but she came in about five minutes later. She came right over to me and said, 'Hello,' and I said, 'Hello.'

"Mr. and Mrs. B——— are very nice people. The house is well kept, has nice furniture. Kathy kept sitting around and talking to me as I pretended to work, until her mother said that, if I didn't want Marjorie bothering me, she would have her go out and play. I told Mrs. B——— that I'd had a daughter once, that she passed on when she was just about Marjorie's age. Kathy didn't say a word, we had our secret.

When I finally left, Kathy walked down the street with me a ways and we agreed we would meet as we had in the dreams —and we set a time each night to try it.

"Oh, yes. I found out that the parents and I knew some of the same people, so it wouldn't be strange or an imposition if I dropped by once in a while. I drop in now and then to see how Kathy is getting along.

"It was a tremendous temptation to tell Mrs. B——— that Kathy/Marjorie was also my daughter. But nothing would have been gained by it. It might have stirred up a lot of grief for everyone if either Kathy or I had a story like that. It probably would have ended up with some professional people coming from around the country and investigating the whole thing. Everyone would know about it, and who knows what the reaction would have been on Kathy, on her folks. No, I gave it a lot of thought, and Kathy and I have agreed to keep it quiet.

"The first time I met with Kathy, in the dream, she was four. She is now seven. We don't meet as frequently as we did. I still do the dreaming, project myself into a scene, sometimes right at her house; but, as time goes by, we meet less and less. When we do meet and talk in the dreams, she isn't as intensely interested as she was. She is growing up, and I don't know how much longer it will last. She seems to be forgetting a lot of the things she remembered when she was Kathy. I've done a lot of reading on the subject of reincarnation since this happened, and it seems that as people who remember their past lives get older, the memory fades. I guess it's just as well.

"She has her own life to live as the girl known as Marjorie. I know, she knows, and maybe it will come out some day when she is older and it won't make such a sensation—when people have gotten to the point where acceptance of this type of thing won't be so unusual."

There were still dozens of questions I would have liked to ask Martin, but somehow they seemed unimportant. I had the core of the story, with a lot of apple around it. I had been sitting with a man who did what he calls dreaming true, out-of-body travel, and in his projections he is convinced he meets with a girl who is the reincarnation of his daughter, and who also does out-of-body travel.

Martin was certainly correct on one point. The more exposure most people have to the unusual, the odd, the occult, the more acceptance they develop to encompass it.

15

I Can't Stay Long

"I can't stay long."

The girl who uttered those words had been dead for over seventeen years! She was speaking through the lips of the girl she was using as her instrument of possession. The phenomenal incident occurred in 1878, in the small town of Watseka, Illinois, about seventy miles from Bloomington, where I was born.

Mary Roff, the excarnate girl, died in 1865. Lurancy Vennum, the possessed girl, was fifteen months old when Mary died, and was almost fourteen years old when Mary returned and took up residence in Lurancy's physical body.

In June of 1970 I had occasion to fly to Chicago. As it had been a long time since I'd visited my numerous relatives in Bloomington, I boarded a shuttle plane and we hedge-hopped the 130 miles back down Route 66. Once with the kinfolk we concocted a clan dinner. During the festivities I asked, "Who knows a ghost, or someone who has reincarnated?"

I listened to a flock of tales, and the one that intrigued me enormously was a recap of what had happened in Watseka so many years ago. Yes, I'd heard of the incident. Being only seventy miles from the site of the event, and having about three days before I had to be back in California, I borrowed a car and drove to Watseka, put up at a motel, and began asking questions.

The answers weren't long in coming; one person recommending another who might know more; someone who had a relative whose father had known the families of the two girls. I pieced the story together from all the verbal sources and researched the records, of which there are many because the case was an international cause célèbre, written up in journals here and abroad.

Mary Roff, a girl almost nineteen in 1865, had what in those days were called fits of insanity. The Roffs were extremely distressed by their daughter's condition, and finally were put in touch with Dr. E. W. Stevens of Janesville, Wisconsin, who had some knowledge of the condition. There wasn't much Dr. Stevens could accomplish with the drugs and medications then available, but he was interested in Mary from the standpoint of split and disturbed personalities, delusive and hysterical behavior.

During her fits, Mary was said to be clairvoyant and clairaudient, known for her powers of divination, which would sometimes last for days. During one of her more violent moments of despondency she cut herself severely on the arm, causing scars that she carried for the rest of her life. Also, during those periods, she could be blindfolded and yet thread needles, sew, and write. Her hands seemed to be independent entities over which she had no conscious control. Mary passed on in 1865, during one of her seizures.

The story picks up on February 1, 1878, with another girl, Lurancy Vennum, who was about fifteen months old when Mary Roff died, and again Dr. Stevens was contacted. (Most of this story has been culled from the writings of Dr. Stevens and other notes made during his personal handling of the case.) Sometime in July 1877 Lurancy, now almost fourteen years old, entered into what appeared to be a sort of fit and remained unconscious for about five hours. She recovered, but had another fit the following day, during which she described to her family the visions she was having—she said she could see heaven, sisters and a brother who had died, heard music and saw angels, and brought communication from those in the spirit world. The fits became more like trance sessions in which she might become highly ecstatic, claiming to be in heaven, seeing all the wondrous sights extolled in biblical stories of the other side. The Vennums seriously considered placing Lurancy in an insane asylum—the existence of a vegetable in those days

But luckily the parents of Mary Roff heard about Lurancy, and got her father to agree to meet with Dr. Stevens. He first met Lurancy in the latter part of January 1878, at a point when she was in a detached attitude of despondency, alternately taking on the general mien and behavior of a crabbed old crone, figuratively spitting at people if they came close to her, calling her parents such names as Old Black Dick for her father, Old Granny for her mother. Dr. Stevens took his time and must have struck a rapport somewhere within Lurancy, as she would talk to him, feeling he wasn't a threat. Under questioning, she described herself as a woman named Kate Hogan; then the personality changed to one distinctly masculine, and she said she was a man named Willie Canning, giving much information about each of the personalities as they surfaced, but losing all knowledge of the previous personality when she took on the next one.

Dr. Stevens was adept at hypnosis, and Lurancy finally agreed to be hypnotized. She then told him she was controlled by excarnate spirits who came and went without her knowing which one would be next. She said the spirits were all bad or evil. Dr. Stevens asked her if it wouldn't be better if she picked a nice spirit to come to her. After some lengthy silence Lurancy said that a girl, Mary Roff, wanted to come and stay in her, and that Mary was nice and wouldn't harm her.

Mr. Roff, who was present during this session, immediately said, "That's my daughter, Mary! Let her come. We will be glad to see her and she will be nice." He added that Mary had also been sick, like Lurancy, and would understand. Lurancy then lapsed into silence, and for all intents and purposes the session was at an end.

Sometime the following day, February 1, Lurancy's father visited Mr. Roff and told him, "Lurancy is now saying she is your daughter, Mary, and she seems real homesick. She wants to see you and her mother and her brothers and sister."

Mr. Roff discussed the situation with the members of his family. It was decided that, if indeed Mary was present in the body of Lurancy, they might bring her to their house. The Roffs, along with Mary's sister Minerva, went to the Vennum house. When they were ushered in, they were told that Lurancy had seen them coming down the street and said, "There comes my ma and my sister, Nervie"—which is the nickname Mary had called Minerva when she was alive. When they all got together, Lurancy was so much like Mary that they were all crying excitedly like a family that had been separated for a long time and now was back together. The Roffs didn't immediately take the girl, who obviously was now their daughter Mary, home with them. "Mary" was now docile and well mannered, exhibiting none of the insane traits she'd had during the periods preceding her death. It was a few days later that the Roffs did take Lurancy into their home as their daughter—and at her insistence they called her Mary.

When Mary met each member of the family, it was with manifestations of deep love, recognition, and identification of each by such personal memories and anecdotes that she was at once accepted by everyone with no doubt, no hesitation. She also said, "I can't stay long. The angels will let me stay until sometime in May," which would give her something over three months with the Roffs.

Not only did she remember each and every member of the family, but she recognized friends, neighbors, and acquaintances whom she'd known in the years prior to her death thirteen years earlier. And there were hundreds of intimate personal memories of which only Mary would have had knowledge. The Roffs were convinced, but they still wanted more proof, so they would place around the house clothing or objects that Mary had either made, or handled frequently during life, and Mary immediately remembered them, in some instances telling the history of some piece of clothing she had made when in life. One time she was talking with someone who'd never heard of the incident of slashing her arm with a knife, and when she began to roll up her sleeve to show the scar, she stopped and said, "This is not the arm; that one is in the ground," and then went on to say where she was buried, and who had been in attendance at the funeral, and so forth.

According to the pamphlet written by Dr. Stevens, Mary said that she spent much time with the doctor's children who were on the other side, giving their correct names and identifying them in other ways. Word of the Mary Roff/Lurancy Vennum phenomenon naturally got out, and it wasn't long before it went national, then international, with men of science and philosophy making the trip to Watseka to test, observe, interview the family, relatives, everyone who might possibly have a tidbit of information or evidence to offer. That evidence was monumental in favor of the transition or possession—that Mary Roff had indeed taken up residence in the person of Lurancy Vennum and was continuing to live in Lurancy's body. Although Mary was *aware* she was in the body of Lurancy, she had no other knowledge of her.

Here are just a few of the memories Mary had of her previous life:

1. How she had slashed her arm with a knife—that arm was "in the ground."

2. The nickname of her sister—"Nervie."

3. The piano in the house, which had been in another house she'd lived in prior to her death.

4. A certain headdress she'd worn prior to her death.

5. Knowing where she'd stayed in Peoria, Illinois, when her folks took her for a water cure.

6. Pointing out on her own arm the place where her brother had been burned by a hot stovepipe.

7. Exact memories of where and how a pet dog had met its death.

8. Remembrance and recognition of the house she had lived and died in, which was different from the one the Roffs lived in while she was with them in Lurancy's body.

9. Remembrance of the maiden name of a former school teacher.

The list could go on and on. The researchers came away convinced, almost to a man, of the authenticity of the phenomenon. Dr. Richard Hodgson, a man of brilliant intellect and education, the keenest and most critical investigator, and a contemporary of that savant parapsychologist, F. W. H. Myers, arrived in Watseka and examined virtually all the witnesses. He substantiated the findings, particularly those of Dr. Stevens, who by this time had published his material in *The Religio-Philosophical Journal* (American spiritualistic weekly founded in 1865, published in Chicago).

Finally came the month of May, and it was time for Mary to return to her own home, to revert to Lurancy Vennum. It was as tearful and loving a parting as the meeting had been. Mary said that her angels told her it was time to go. Mr. Roff drove Mary back to the Vennums' house in a buggy, and by the time they arrived there, the transition was complete—Mary Roff had departed; Lurancy Vennum was once again back in herself. She thanked Mr. Roff for his family's kindness. Upon meeting her own folks, she recognized them and was the warm, friendly daughter they'd known before she started having fits.

After returning home, Lurancy would occasionally have conversations with Mary, chatting on like old friends, asking and answering questions. Lurancy developed into a trance medium for a time; in those states Mary Roff would come through and converse with her parents and friends.

Lurancy lived a happy and well-balanced life, not exhibiting any of the former tendencies of split or disordered personality she'd had prior to the control by Mary. Lurancy grew to womanhood and married a farmer named George Binning, who knew nothing of spiritualism or psychic phenomena and was constantly amazed at the revelations emitting from Lurancy during the periods when Mary would come through. Dr. Richard Hodgson, as a final case note, wrote:

> I have no doubt that the incidents occurred substantially as described in the narrative by Dr. Stevens, and in my view the only other interpretation of the case, besides the spiritistic, that seems at all plausible is that which has been put forward as the alternative to the spiritistic theory to account for the trance-communications of Mr. Piper [a trance medium of then international reknown] and similar cases, viz., secondary personality with supernormal powers. It would be difficult to disprove this hypothesis in the case of the Watseka Wonder, owing to the comparative meagerness of the record and the probable abundance of "suggestion" in the environment, and any conclusion that we may reach would probably be determined largely by our convictions concerning other cases. My personal opinion is that the Watseka Wonder case belongs in the main manifestations to the spiritistic category.*

It is interesting to note the age of the entity manifesting the phenomenon—between twelve and seventeen years of age, which parapsychologists have concluded is the time when extreme personality changes or disorders occur, particularly in the female. I've been advised time and again, in my continuing search for the unexplained, to be on the lookout for adolescents, who usually aren't even aware they are causing phenomena.

Did Mary Roff return via the instrument of Lurancy Vennum? How did she accomplish it? Nobody knows.

* F. W. H. Myers, *Human Personality and Its Survival of Bodily Death* (New York: University Books, 1961), pp. 71–72.

16

This Time I Am an Indian

When I flew to Albuquerque, New Mexico, on Friday, May 24, 1974, to attend a metaphysics conference, there was no thought in my mind I would be fortunate enough to be placed in contact with a man who gave me recollections of an experience he had as a cavalry officer. During that lifetime he had been killed in a battle in the Texas Panhandle just about one hundred years ago.

There were a total of about five hundred people attending the conference of whom two hundred were in attendance at the opening session. A number of them knew of my wide interest in and writing on subjects concerning the paranormal, so they weren't surprised when I began asking around if anyone present had reincarnative recollections, experiences, or knew of someone who did. I drew a blank until I sat with a group of Indians attending the conference. Right off I explained the type of stories I was looking for, and they understood immediately what I was after. One of them knew of a man who was visiting in Albuquerque, from Ruidoso, New Mexico, a town some 125 miles southeast of Albuquerque, and the man had talked about having lived a former life.

When you listen to a person who has a reincarnative recollection, if you have any imagination at all, the emotions evoked make you a party to the incident. When Gregory, a Mescalero Apache, sat in my room at the Hilton Inn and told me what he had experienced in another life, I felt I was living through the experience with him.

Gregory (not his real name) and some friends had taken a trip into the northwest section of the Texas Panhandle. He pointed out on a map the approximate location he was talking about but otherwise professed to know nothing of its history concerning Indian–cavalry skirmishes or battles.

Gregory is thirty-four years old. He does not live on the Indian reservation at Ruidoso but lives nearby and works in Ruidoso. He took the hunting trip to the Texas Panhandle about four years ago with two friends.

"We parked our camper by the dirt road at this place and walked about a mile from it. We were separated, about a hundred feet apart. I was just walking along, carrying my rifle. All at once I stopped and I couldn't move. I began to breathe heavy, you know. I hadn't been running, so there wasn't any reason I should be breathing that way, and I'm in pretty good shape anyway. Then I began to feel dizzy. It scared me, but I didn't know what to do. I just stood there. Then I began to hear things.

"It was like people shouting, like they were excited. There were many voices, many people. Then I heard horses running, and then guns going off. Then I began to see things. I saw people but they were hazy. They were on horseback and they were shouting. There were other people. Some were Indians and some were white men riding horses. Those white men must have been soldiers, because they had on uniforms and hats. Everybody was shooting rifles and pistols. I looked down at myself, and I saw that I had on boots and the legs of my blue pants were stuffed in the boots. I didn't see the color of my shirt, but I knew I had a hat on. The rifle I had in my hands then was not the same rifle I was carrying on the hunting trip. It was a shorter rifle and I remember bringing it to my shoulder and firing and the kick was bigger than my own rifle I had with me. There was a lot of confusion and I could feel myself begin to run. All at once I heard a gunshot, I felt myself get hit, and then I began to fall. I guess that is when I got it, got hit, and that is how it ended."

I asked if he felt the actual impact of the bullet hitting him.

"I felt something like a punch. It didn't hurt too much, but I knew I had been shot, and then I began to fall down. That was all. I think I died then. I don't remember anything else, just that."

"Who do you think you were in that life, at that time?"

"Seeing the blue pants and the high boots I was wearing, and that rifle—well, I think I was a white officer. I do remember hearing myself shouting orders. I don't remember what they were, but I was shouting orders to the men to do something."

"Do you remember seeing people who looked like Indians; were people dressed as in those days?"

"Sort of, but not definitely. Some people had on clothes and some of them didn't have on so much. The people who were yelling, making a lot of noise, I think were Indians. And I think an Indian shot me. I remember breathing very hard, and then I was moving forward, and I got shot and I began staggering like I was going to fall. One of my friends said later he saw me staggering around so he came running over to see if I was all right.

"The other guy came over, and I told them what I had just felt and seen. They seemed to understand and they just looked at me."

Interestingly, Greg was quite specific about where he was shot. When I asked, he indicated his left side. "On the side, right here. I have done some boxing and it felt just like when a guy will hit you real hard right there, a hard punch, enough to knock you down."

"Did you know of or ever hear of a Indian–cavalry fight in that area, at any time in the past?"

"No. I know the Indians and the soldiers had some fights in a lot of places, but I don't know if anything happened right there."

Greg summed up the experience this way: "If this is true, maybe I was a white officer, a soldier, in some other life. I was in a fight with Indians and I got shot and killed. That would be funny, wouldn't it? I maybe shot Indians in that life, chased them and shot them. In this life I am an Indian. Things are different now, we don't have battles like that anymore. I guess maybe I had to come back in this life as an Indian to see how it feels."

When I returned home the first order of business was to transcribe the tape of the above interview. The next point was to try to ascertain if and when any Indian–cavalry battles might have been fought in that particular area. A couple of research books later the only possibility I have been able to pin down was what was known as the battle of Adobe Walls, June 27, 1874. That battle launched a warrior named Quanah Parker, of the Kwahari Comanche. His mother was Cynthia Ann Parker, a white girl who had been captured by the Indians in 1836. When she was recaptured by the whites in 1860 she hardly knew her real name, had few recollections of her childhood as the white girl she had been born. She was the wife of a Chief, her son Quanah went on to become a great Chief of the Comanche.

The soldiers who took part in that fight at Adobe Walls were under the command of Colonel Kit Carson. He was commanding 335 New Mexico and California volunteers and seventy-five Ute and Apache allies. Estimates are that Carson's troops were up against from one to three thousand Indians, and he was forced to withdraw. Carson and many of the troops used the Hawkens rifle, but many others had the smaller bore, shorter rifle, the Sharps Breechloading Percussion Single-shot Carbine, manufactured in calibers from .32 to .52, delivering four to five shots a minute. The rifle Gregory was carrying at the time of his experience in this life was of .22 caliber, hardly big enough to administer that "kick" he felt when he fired the "other" rifle.

Yes, there had been an Indian–cavalry fight in the area where Gregory and his companions were hunting. Undoubtedly a number of Kit Carson's troops were killed, among them possibly some officers.

The other possibility that must be considered with Gregory's story is that of a possible replay of the Memory Tape Of Time. A battle did take place there in 1874; at the time Gregory and his friends stopped in the area conditions were just right for that replay to occur atmospherically, although it was only *seen* by Gregory.

But what gives added impetus to the reincarnative hypothesis in this case is that Gregory was *himself,* the individual in the battle, a soldier who was engaged in the fight, and was shot, by exactly whom he doesn't know, and he feels he was killed at that time.

Did he or didn't he? Was it or wasn't it? It is quite a picturesque waking recollection and experience.

PART IV
Trance and Spirit Communication

17

I Was a Primitive Man

I was thoroughly captivated by a man who said he'd lived 250,000 years ago. I've heard a great many of these thousands-of-years-ago stories and had no reason to believe this one would be much different—until I heard it, that is.

Actually, Roger's story should be titled "He Went Back." It seems that is what he has done, to the utter consternation and confusion of the researchers, including psychiatrists, paleontologists, archeologists, paleotropicists, and paleobotanists, to say nothing of students of the Bible.

I first met Roger in the office of the Southern California Society for Psychical Research.

A week after we met, I went to an apartment building in Venice, California, to get the details of his story. I knocked on the door marked Manager, and was invited in by a good-looking man, vigorous of action, quick and expressive with his hands. One of the first questions I asked him was his birthdate. He said it was October 2, 1897. I would have sworn he was only in his fifties.

Here is his story:

"My name is Roger, and I had an experience that has lasted most of my life—that is, I've lived with it and have gone into variations of the experience. I go through what can only be called a trance state, and not only have I accumulated a vast amount of surprising information in this manner but I've also talked with any number of psychiatrists, anthropologists, paleontologists, and have familiarized myself with much more data that is related to it in a purely scientific manner.

"One of the first men of science to become interested in me was one of the prominent psychiatrists at the famous Nuremberg trials after World War II. I met him when he was associated with the New York Psychiatric Institute in New York City. From him, I learned a number of things, all of which were scientifically related to the remote period of my story. After this psychiatrist investigated me, I heard the same things from other researchers who had no knowledge of my experiences.

"The human brain, or any animal brain, is different from the rest of the body because, in the course of evolution, many parts of the body such as our appendix, our bones, have become atrophied, or have been made useless, and are finally cast aside, changed, reworked, like the little toe, which is probably vanishing. But the brain doesn't change; otherwise we wouldn't be able to see, hear, feel, or have balance. And now we find that plants and insects have a living intelligence. Our brain contains all the information it ever possessed, or rather, the soul coming into a new body brings all that memory and it is activated within the new brain—except that the information is largely suppressed, censored. From time to time something will happen to cough up a piece of buried information, which amazes us and makes us think we are going nutty. It has been explained to me that the new cells grow over the already existing cells and, shall we say, cover up the previous knowledge or information that is brought in already contained within the soul-brain, but that knowledge is still there and is called the subconscious. As we progress from life to life, a whole new set of circumstances prevails; our brain doesn't change, except to grow larger, which it is doing. But new experiences are added and they divert us from the past memory into new channels, so new sets of cells come into being and begin to pick up their own knowledge and experience in the present moment of Earthly existence. How many new sets of circumstances have we experienced since we came into being as humans, or even before?

"You begin to get the idea. It's eternal, and that is how long we've been accumulating information—that is, the brain change from life to life. At the present time we have a very highly developed cerebral cortex, and you've also noted how much more advanced man has become in his thinking in just the last fifty years—more advancement than he made in thousands of years.

"What is necessary to get back into the past, and I mean perhaps hundreds to thousands of years ago, is to temporarily suspend the brain from present activity. Then the individual consciousness will be that of our remote ancestors, because we actually are our remote ancestor, updated."

From what Roger had already touched on, I knew that what was coming would probably be enough to make me hook up on the static line for a 250,000-year leap into the past.

"Well, it isn't exactly known how this remote memory can be uncovered, brought out, but they know that it can be done, that it's feasible.

"Without actually knowing what I was doing, I accomplished that breakthrough. I did it through stark fright and hopelessness—you might call it morbidity. I was only twenty-seven at the time of this revelation, young compared to my age now. I won't go into the details of what brought me to that state of mind, but let me say it was traumatic. At the time, I was nobody, I was nothing; it didn't really matter what happened to me, I thought. It seems as though something like that is almost essential at times to induce the sort of thing that happened to me.

"It was then that I began to think what I would do, really do, if I were the only person left on this planet. Many people ask themselves that question, but they only ask it superficially. I put myself into a state of mind where I *believed* I was completely alone, the only person on Earth. You can imagine my state of mind when I tell you that I spent literally days on end concentrating on being the only person alive. I carried this on long enough so that I walked around in a half daze, hardly knowing what I was doing. I would sometimes sit for two or three hours visualizing it, becoming familiar with the feeling of being completely alone, until it became normal and natural to me. I lived it.

"One night, after a period of long concentration, actually going into a trance state, I heard a voice say, 'Don't do that! You'll go crazy. Don't believe that!' That shook me a good deal. The voice was just as real as you and I sitting here talking. It was a moment of real and terrible fear, but I didn't care. As I say, I was nobody, I had nothing, and I just didn't care. So I went ahead with my concentration. I felt for a moment as if I were holding onto a rod over a dark pit, not knowing at all what was under me, what I would fall into. The willingness to let go, regardless of how you feel, is hard. So I held on to the rod and kept on with my fantasy; I was in a sort of fury to keep going. It was almost as if something took possession of me, was using me as an experimental instrument.

"All at once I knew I was the only person on this planet.

"It probably only lasted a few seconds. I saw myself rushing out on a field, and there wasn't a living thing but me. If you have a strong imagination, you will know the great terror that seized me. Then I saw a tree in the field. I rushed over to it and threw my arms around the trunk, trying to make contact with some living thing—even though it wasn't human, it was alive—trying to make myself a part of that living tree. That was the only thing I could become one with. That was the first step. The hallucination or fantasy dissolved then; I came out of it, but I was amazed at the success I had. Then my enthusiasm scared me. The next time I did this, I mentally took a woman along with me because I found out I didn't want to be the *only* living human being on Earth. I was making some progress. I only took her on that one trip, as I found she didn't contribute that much. I don't mean that in any derogatory sense about women; I like them very much. It's just that, after I took a woman on the trip, I found I didn't really need anyone with me. A psychiatrist I told this part of the story to asked me if we had sexual intercourse on the trip, and I had to disappoint him. In fact it never occurred to me. I just wanted her along for company.

"After that it didn't take me as long as before to get into that former state. I was learning the knack the hard way, I guess. The extreme fear about doing it wasn't there. My mind responded to my wishing and gave me the aura of complete conviction that I had returned to some place I had known. When I was in that trance state, it seemed there was a little string attached from me back to my consciousness, the physical me. I seemed to know this return was happening in India —and it was just as if I had never been anywhere but India. And then, too, on this particular trip I saw a woman, not the woman I had taken with me before, but a different one, and she lived there—so I wasn't the only living human being. In fact there was some connection between this woman and me, some family or relative connection.

"The woman was just standing there when I first saw her, in the desert, with some brush in her hands, as though she'd been gathering firewood, I guess. And then she looked up and saw me. She started toward me, and I hurriedly began backing up. For some reason I was terrified because she was a woman. The reason for this, as I found out later, is that it was a matriarchal society. The woman, the childbearer, reigned supreme and the man was subject to her. So I knew she was superior to me in that life—she was my boss. This is diametrically opposed to my feeling in my present life. Anyway, she walked steadily toward me and I actually got on my knees and pleaded with her not to hurt me. She had a large branch in her hand, and as she approached me she raised it high over her head and—whomp! I guess she hit me with it and killed me because I went out like a light and have never had another trip like that particular one—nor did I ever see that woman again, thank goodness.

"When I took those trips I was back there, I seemed to have tapped a remote section of the brain, or the memory had just surfaced under the proper conditions and revealed memories of a primitive life in which I was a primitive man among primitive people.

"The people who have worked with me on this are generally agreed that I lived about 250,000 years ago. Now that had to be an inherited memory from some source other than this present world, where things are not a bit like what I have described and will describe. As far as the archeologists and paleontologists can figure out, this whole sequence took place right on, or near the Great Indian Desert. There was no such name then. It was hotter at that time, too, by ten or fifteen degrees. It's a very old section of the planet. They've found petrified dinosaur eggs there. There were sand dunes and rocks and caves and small isolated pools of water surrounded by trees and vegetation. We ate among other things, insects, watercress, roots—anything that would sustain life. I never felt as if I had ever been anywhere else, just there on the desert, completely at home, knowing the environment and living with it. Each time I put myself into what amounted to the trance state, I would always return to the same place, the same period of time, and the scenes continued, very clear and very logical. What's baffled the scientists and psychiatrists who've worked with me is that I have such a detailed memory of this. A certain professor at the University of Southern California wanted to know where I had gotten the information, what degrees I had, where I had studied. When I told him my educational background, and that I had learned all this in a trance state, he got furious and asked me a lot of questions, most of which I answered right off—questions about the period and the people. That made him even madder. He finally pointed his finger at the door and ordered me to get out before he called the police and had me put away as a nut."

That last statement by Roger immediately put me in mind of Dr. Jules Eisenbud, the researcher who investigated and wrote extensively about Ted Serios, the man who projects thought pictures onto unexposed film by mind power. Dr. Eisenbud called a professor who had previously started some work with Ted and then dropped it. Dr. Eisenbud asked him why he'd stopped working with Ted. The professor reportedly answered, "I asked Mr. Serios for a certain thought picture on the film and he gave me another one not even related!" The scientist dropped him because he didn't project the *right* pictures.

But as for Roger, I asked for more descriptions, such as the kind of clothing, or covering, he wore in those days.

"I didn't wear anything," he answered. "Let me qualify that. I wore, we wore, strips of bark on our backs and on our feet when we went out in the sun. When we were out on the hunt for food, we didn't walk upright, rather, we sort of loped, like apes, you might say. We put on the bark, and pulled off long bunches of dry grass, like straw, and carried them in our mouths, like a sort of camouflage. Man hunted man, and we did practice cannibalism then, but of course there was nothing wrong with it; there was no sense of it being illegal and immoral; meat was meat. We usually wouldn't eat people of our own group, but we sure did dine on the people of neighboring groups or hostile groups that attacked us.

"We had horses then, too. I learned a lot about how we hunted horses when I returned in the trance state, although I hadn't asked to be shown that specifically. A number of us would surround a bunch of horses, and we would isolate a laggard and drive it into a boggy area, a wallow area, where it would sink down to its knees in mud. Now you've heard that ancient man used sharp rocks for cutting things. That's true, except when we hunted horses we didn't use weapons of any kind, just ourselves. We outflanked the animal, and when it got into the bog we would hurl ourselves on it. By dint of strength and tearing at its jugular with our teeth, we opened up the vein and drank the blood. Then we would haul the horse out and bury the carcass in the hot sand. In a few days, when we went back and uncovered it, the animal would have been cooked to a turn in that sand oven; it was no trouble to strip off the flesh and eat it. We didn't need weapons to do that. Everyone cooked his meat that way. When we were away from our own group and found a mound of sand, we knew what was under it and would steal whatever kind of animal, or man, had been buried, to eat it.

"Not too many years ago, when I moved out here to California with my wife, we went to the Pomona County Fair. While we were walking around looking at the exhibits, I saw a large photograph of a horse on the front of one of the exhibit buildings. I immediately knew that horse. It was the same type we had chased and used for food in the desert. It didn't look like a Shetland pony; it was quite dark, larger than a Shetland but smaller than the horses of today.

"Racially, we were slightly Oriental. Not Chinese, nor Mongols, but Oriental, definitely. Our skin was pale yellow, but most of us were burned black by the terrific heat and the constant exposure to the sun. The Berbers and the Bedouins, those who live out in the desert today, have somewhat the same coloring we had then, but we were darker and we didn't look exactly like either of those types.

"When I first worked with the doctor I mentioned, I told him about some of these things. He started investigating me, as any psychiatrist would, to see if it could be explained by psychoanalytical methods. He tried to find out if by some means I had heard about such things when I was a child and the memory had gone into my subconscious. He couldn't uncover any hidden memory that would account for the things I was coming up with. He tried every method he could think of to break down the story. As you can imagine, I've not had any wide acceptance of my story.

"I've gotten used to being looked at as though I'm a nut; it doesn't bother me anymore! The psychiatrist told me I would be looked on as a kook, but not to let it bother me because people just can't understand anything that defies analysis or is out of the ordinary. His explanation for what I've been through was that I'd had a reawakening of a dormant portion of my brain, and the memory came flooding back when I was in the trance state. Somehow that memory ploughed its way up through the layers of memory of other lives. I've never had any memories, either awake or in trance, of any period other than the one on the desert. Other psychiatrists have tried to get me to go into other lives, at times with hypnosis, but I've not been able to.

"In those early days of research, the doctor did try to hook things up through old writings, legends, and myths that would lend some credence—like the Bible, the Talmud, the Koran, old scrolls. I remember that 250,000 years ago we didn't know exactly how babies come into being. We knew there were males and females because each was built differently, but we didn't know anything much about sex, except it felt good when you had an orgasm; you just did it when you wanted to. When storms came, as they frequently did, and do, out there, we would hole up in our caves and about the only thing we had to pass the time with was sex. We came to the conclusion that babies had something to do with storms; we thought that when the wind blew there would be babies.

"Aside from these instances of returning to the desert, I've never had any psychic or supernormal experiences. What would be to gain if I did? I'm in my seventies now, and if I'd wanted to make money or a name for myself I would have tried a lot harder, pushed myself in bizarre ways as many frauds do today. I just want to try to find out what's going on."

There was no self-pity, no resentment in Roger. He is brimming with vitality and enjoys life. He has accepted his niche in this life. He and his wife are managing the apartment building. During my session people would knock on the door of his office, poke their heads in, and inquire about apartments for rent or just stop by to say hello. I must admit that, as he related his story, my mind would at times balk and jump and I would try to think of some way to trick him, asking him questions that could destroy the whole thing.

When I told Roger I thought I had heard enough, far from being downcast, he popped up from the couch like a young man, and thanked me profusely for giving him my time to get the story. As he let me out the front door of the apartment building, I couldn't help doing some marveling. He actually lives in two worlds—the one of the present and the one of antiquity. And he has left us the legacy of what he related here.

18

Just Call Me Ulysses

Dr. Freda Morris called and gave me the name of a man who worked with Paramount Studio. She made no comment other than "Ron has something *very* interesting; you'll like it." I called Ron and set up a lunch meeting at Oblath's Restaurant, across the street from the studio. Paramount is where I started in films, so the moment I walked in I was flooded with memories of other lunches with Veronica Lake, Billy DeWolf, Ray Milland, Gail Russell, Bob Preston.

What I got from Ron were the results of hypnotic sessions he'd held with a twenty-year-old man. They had tried age regression. What happened was that an excarnate popped up and, speaking through the youth, said he had lived three different lifetimes recently, but at the present time he was "watching over the youth, was part of him."

Ron and his subject had been trying to find out if the boy had lived a former life.

Here's how Ron's sessions went:

"I wasn't very involved in the whole area of psychic phenomena at the time. I was strictly playing around with hypnosis. And I'd better add here that I'm not an expert in hypnosis by any means. I'd been doing it for a number of years as a sort of parlor game, and from what I've learned in the meantime I would also like to add a warning. Hypnosis should really be done only by a trained analyst, someone who knows what he is dealing with, because it can be dangerous under certain circumstances. You never know when one of those circumstances will arise during a session, or even later as the result of it. The subject can freak out.

"I became interested in the subject of age regression after reading a book about a group of people in Boulder, Colorado, who wanted to do the same thing, except perhaps go further. There were six people in that group. They put a housewife into hypnosis and were able to take her back. They got some age regression, and also very explicit, detailed explanations of a past life this woman had supposedly lived. Then they took her, in that past life, forward to the moment of her death, then beyond that moment of death to see where she was. Apparently, under hypnosis the woman, after the moment of death, experienced an in-between state that turned out to be without personality yet totally knowledgeable in the sense of being aware of what the universe was, what man was, what life was, why she had lived that life, and why she was going to live another life soon. She discussed everything with clergymen, scientists, and researchers, giving details she had no way of knowing in her waking or present-day life. She talked about reincarnation and said it was a fact; she explained the state she was in, the reason for her living a series of lives, and—as well as she could in words—the nature of God. The key point was the idea of one universal mind.

"One day, while I was working for a photograph concern in Hollywood and still doing postgraduate work at UCLA, I met a young fellow who was then twenty. We were working the same job together, and we got to discussing hypnosis. It turned out he was interested in being hypnotized, though he'd never tried it. We made arrangements for him to come to my place so I could try to hypnotize him. His name is Carl. He did go under, very deeply. He turned out to be an excellent subject. We did a number of basic hypnosis experiments with visual hallucination, audible hallucination, and so on. Then we started experimenting with age regression, within his own life. He went deeper and deeper every time we experimented. There was a particular thing in his early childhood he wanted to find out about. He would keep going back to that point, but there was great resistance when we got to it. Obviously there was something in him that didn't want to uncover whatever it was. He persisted. I didn't want to play around with that because, as I said, I'm not trained to handle those things. He was asking me to do what an analyst does. So I said, 'I'll go back into your memory gently. If you start resisting, I'll stop.' One day when I was taking him back, exploring this area he wanted to know about, and suddenly a voice with a very different sound to it, and with great authority, said, 'Stop it. I don't want you going into Carl's past!'

"That pretty well shook me! This was Carl talking, supposedly, but with a different voice. It even sounded like another person.

"I didn't know what else to do, so I asked the voice, 'Who are you?'

"Immediately, just as though we were carrying on a conversation, which I guess we were, it said, 'You know who I am.'

"I said, 'No I don't. Would you explain?'

"It said, 'I'm working through the force.'

" 'What do you mean, the force?'

" 'I'm working through that which is Carl, which moves Carl; I am working through what you would call the soul, the spirit, and through the subconscious.'

" 'Why are you talking to me through Carl?'

" 'Because of your desire for it, and to protect Carl if you go too far.'

" 'Who are you? I mean, are you somebody who can be identified?'

" 'Yes, but who I am is not important.'

" 'It is to me, and perhaps also to Carl. Are you someone

who is alive, or have been alive—I mean, have you lived before?'

" 'Yes.'

" 'Where?'

" 'Here on Earth. In my last life I was an attorney in the Midwest. I have lived other lifetimes; everyone has.'

" 'What was your name?'

" 'It is none of your business. It is not important.'

" 'Why can't you identify yourself?' I asked.

" 'It would make certain living people unhappy. They do not believe; they have never believed.'

" 'Do you have a name? What should I call you?'

"There was a moment's hesitation, then, 'Just call me Ulysses.'

" 'You mean, the Ulysses of . . . ?'

" 'Not the Ulysses you are thinking of—just Ulysses. You asked me for a name. Do not think of me as a personality. I have no personality now. I will later when I return into physical life again.'

" 'What are you doing talking through Carl?' I went on.

" 'In my present state I can work with the force in and through Carl. Think of me as the true Carl. Carl is an entity, I am an entity—that remains constant in each incarnation. When the physical body dies, the personality disappears; only the force remains.'

" 'How can you work through Carl? I mean, how do you work through someone else?'

" 'I become the force working through Carl; at the same time I am the entire force. It is a paradox. The individual force within a man is at the same time the overall force of the universe. It cannot be explained in words. I approximate it for you. Right now, think of two circles: Carl is the outer circle, I am the inner circle, working from within the larger circle.'

" 'Can you tell me . . .'

" 'That is all for now. You must not tire the entity. You may work through Carl, but you must not overdo it. If you disturb him too much, I shall make you stop.' "

Trance and Spirit Communication

Now that I was all built up, in the middle of a fascinating mystery, it just *couldn't* be over! I said as much to Ron, and he smiled at me as he casually took another bite of a huge salad the waitress had placed before him. I pushed him, "That's all? That's it?"

"Oh, no. That was just the first session with Ulysses. The next sessions we had with Ulysses were the ones I taped, and there were other people present at the time. They can verify the things I've told you, because I had Ulysses repeat what he said in that first session, when Carl and I were alone and I hadn't taped it."

Subsequently, I read all the transcriptions reportedly emanating from Ulysses, and I listened to the tapes, and felt they should be written up, or at least pertinent parts. To try to get it all in would be a book in itself, and some of it gets pretty deeply into subjects that only scientists could understand. The following is a portion of the fourth session held through the medium of Carl, attended by Ron and two friends on July 21, 1963:

ULYSSES: . . . I said that I feel light. What I meant was that light is an energy that is used as you use food. This feeds the force. The force could not exist without light. Light comes from the sun and is not made on Earth.

RON: Is the light from the sun the only source that the force feeds on?

ULYSSES: It is the closest.

RON: Then it is strictly the fact that you are living in a physical being that inhabits Earth, therefore you are fed by the light of the sun?

ULYSSES: No, you do not understand. I am not fed by light now. Only as a force.

RON: You mean after the physical body has died?

ULYSSES: That is correct.

RON: You mean that, after the physical body has died, you are still in the physical proximity of the Earth?

ULYSSES: That is correct.

RON: Are there physical forces in the proximity of the other stars?

ULYSSES: I will not answer that question now. Ask it at another time when you have more understanding, when we have built the base.

RON: I see. May I ask some questions?

ULYSSES: Yes. It does not mean that they will be answered.

RON: I have read a lot of accounts. I'm not sure of the validity of all of them. Some of them have supposedly been in various forms of automatic writing, dictated by someone who has passed away from this life. In these accounts these beings, or spirits, or whatever I may call them, have talked of dying physically and then leading a life very similar to the physical plane in which they lived their life—in their former physical surroundings, but with certain changes. For instance, the house they lived in was more perfect, the way they had always wanted it to be. My question is this: Could you tell me specifically what happens at the moment of death? Do you return immediately to a force state, or are there intermediate stages of existence?

ULYSSES: Number one, when, as you say you die, you do not die—only the physical portion ceases to function. You will return to the physical state if there is someone also in the physical state who wishes you to stay there. If there is no one who wishes you to stay, then you will return to the force immediately. The only way you will be kept in a physical force is through the emotion you call love. If someone feels love for you to a great extent, then you will be kept in the physical state until this love dissipates. Then you will go to the force.

RON: I think I understand.

ULYSSES: You do not understand yet, but you will, perhaps later, when you experience the emotions of which I told you. There are other emotions that keep the one who is gone in a physical state, like fear and hate and revenge, and they are bad for everyone.

RON: May I ask another question?

ULYSSES: I told you that you could. I will answer them from the extent of my own knowledge, through Carl.

RON: I have a question about you, yourself, speaking to

Trance and Spirit Communication 169

us. Is everything you say to us to be taken as absolute truth or as an opinion? And also, do you have the ability to lie? Or an inability to die?

ULYSSES: There is no reason to lie to you. What you accept as the truth is up to you. There are no opinions given; there are no lies given. There is no reason for lies.

RON: I wasn't asking whether you did lie, but I was asking whether it was possible for you to do so, let us say for the welfare of Carl, consciously? Then would you be able to lie to us?

ULYSSES: There is no reason to lie. You would just not receive an answer if I did not know it.

RON: I see. I will word this slowly. In being a part of Carl, as you say you are, do you just sort of go along for the ride as he lives his physical life? Or do you have a specific pattern or plan you try to follow or try to influence him? You have said he has free will, but do you have a specific plan in mind for Carl's life?

ULYSSES: There is no specific plan as such by me. There is a specific plan for every life, but the free will gets in the way and it takes many lifetimes to learn to obey, to follow the law. If we could influence specific lives, there would be no crimes.

RON: If you have gone through other experiences, physical experiences here on Earth, why, when you come into another physical existence, is this prior knowledge closed off to the conscious mind? Why is it not part of the conscious? Why do I have to put Carl into a state of hypnosis in order to get this knowledge?

ULYSSES: The knowledge gained by reentering the force from the physical was never meant to be used by man. The conscious part is purely a screen. The subconscious part is aware of the conscious. I possess all knowledge that has been in existence since the beginning of time, as do you. Not all of this can be brought into words for you to understand. If this was done all at once, the conscious mind would burst. It is not capable of receiving and retaining all knowledge consciously. It was not built for that. There is a section that you call memory. The memory is part of the force and the subconscious. Do you understand?

There were other questions by Ron, but the session had ceased abruptly. Carl breathed deeply for a time, then Ron carefully and slowly brought him back to the present and, not knowing just what to leave as memory at this time, told Carl that he would not remember the conversation. Later, when Carl expressed interest, he listened to the tapes of the sessions and was only mildly interested.

This isn't the first time I've heard of those on the other side telling us flatly that something is none of our business, that we wouldn't understand it. It would appear their manner of life is the same but different from our conscious physical manner. We are the low men on the totem pole. One discarnate speaking through an entranced medium said, "We know little more about all this than you do," going on to explain that they do have some knowledge but it's a sort of experimenting on both sides; not everyone here can communicate, and not everyone there can communicate. It's trial and error, at best.

Let's take another portion of a session conducted by Ron with Carl and attended by three other people. One of the questions put to Ulysses concerned theology.

RON: Christians believe there are many signs pointing to the birth of Christ as something greater than man, the son of God, in the sense that . . .

ULYSSES: He was greater than unenlightened man because he tapped the force.

RON: I am talking about the typical Christian belief. For instance, Catholics believe that he is the son of God.

ULYSSES: We all are, if you will think of the force of God.

RON: But Christian religions seem to say that he was more than this, and the average man . . .

ULYSSES: There is no average man. We are all part of the same force. When humans make legends, they do exaggerate.

RON: Is the virgin birth a legend? That Christ was born without Mary having had sexual intercourse with a physical man?

ULYSSES: There is no significance. Only a wish of purity.

RON: Am I to take it that this then is a legend; is that what you are saying?

ULYSSES: A woman must be inseminated. A normal course of laws must take its course.

RON: What about the belief of the physical resurrection of the body of Christ after death?

ULYSSES: Physical?

RON: The fact that the tomb was empty and a spirit or angel was found standing there and said that Christ had gone to his father.

ULYSSES: An angel.

RON: I guess I'm not putting this right, but it is a Christian concept.

ULYSSES: Yes.

RON: Well, it is written that on Easter morning they found an angel there and he said that Christ had risen.

ULYSSES: I believe I mentioned before—the senses can be extended and the years can be formed. In those times such concepts as astral projection, two and two equals four, and so forth, were unknown to the common people. To them this was magic. This is out of the question. When astral projection is done even today, it is deemed black magic by some people, so think what it was like two thousand years ago. The physical body of Christ was disintegrated as a convenience. Many have been taken this way.

RON: And Christ's appearance to the apostles in the upper room—would this be the astral body?

ULYSSES: This was a physical body formed through the process of astral projection and the force. A physical materialization.

RON: Can this be done after death?

ULYSSES: You must remember that Christ was capable of many things because he was able to use the force. Thus, when dying, he was able to do many things, because of his contacting the force. He wished to do certain things before receiving the force himself, after death.

RON: When the apostles, according to the New Testament,

had received the Holy Spirit, they spoke in tongues, what is called glossolalia. This happens today, speaking in foreign or at least unintelligible tongues. Can you tell me what this means? Is it ecstasy when people babble in some other language?

ULYSSES: The force has no language as you know it. There is no need, we do not feel sound.

RON: I don't understand. What would this phenomenon be then?

ULYSSES: Possibly a throwback to an earlier reincarnation.

RON: I was thinking it might be that, or might be a contact by other forces.

ULYSSES: There is no other force, as you put it. It is all one force. If there is no knowledge gained from speaking in tongues, then it is useless. No knowledge, no use. Now you must stop the questioning for the time being. These sessions become very lengthy. You cannot learn everything at once. The best you can do is make a beginning.

Glossolalia, or speaking in tongues, also known as xenoglossis, is the speech of an entranced person in language unfamiliar to his conscious state, and it has been the subject of unresolvable controversy. It seems difficult enough for us to receive straight messages from spirits on the other side; and the problem is remarkably compounded with the addition of utterances emitting from an entranced person and not only purporting to be in a language unknown to the individual but apparently coming from excarnates or discarnates who are said to take over and make the person speak in a language that cannot be, or has not been, understood. It has been suggested that people who gather in groups and raise the power to speak in tongues do so in a collective subliminal fracture brought about by ecstasy or hysteria. The whole subject is speculative.

The last hypnosis session Ron held with Carl was on January 2, 1964, some seven months after they started, at which time five people were present, including the two principals. The questions put to Ulysses had become more pointed, and it is interesting to isolate the portion of the final reading that dealt with a few contemporary problems—alcohol, cigarettes, and pills:

RON: Does drinking alcoholic beverages retard spiritual development?

ULYSSES: Yes.

RON: Tea and coffee?

ULYSSES: This is hard to say since things other than water and milk deal mainly with the physical function of the body. Smoking relaxes and slows down the thinking processes. Alcoholic beverages do this also, only in a much more efficient way. They numb both the nerves and the ability to think correctly. They have a much more lasting effect.

RON: Are there some people for whom drinking or smoking in moderation would be more of a benefit than a detriment, for relaxing?

ULYSSES: You must define what you mean by moderation.

RON: A pack of cigarettes a day. Say in the degree Carl smokes.

ULYSSES: Entirely too much.

RON: A pack a day?

ULYSSES: It depends upon how much tension the individual is under. If this seems to alleviate it—but I cannot say that it is good. Those things taken into the body to relieve tension and anxiety load up the system and must be eliminated. Alcoholic beverages dull the senses and the ability to think correctly. The world that you live in today is a higher materialistic, mechanized world, and you are confronted with problems, and you do not let the force help you. You try to answer all problems by escaping through the use of drugs, narcotics, and the like, which isn't possible.

RON: If a person passes on under the influence of alcohol, does it hamper his entrance into the next plane?

ULYSSES: I stated before that the transition to the next plane is not immediate, and the person must first realize he is deceased and proceed from there.

RON: If he dies under the influence of alcohol, is this more difficult?

ULYSSES: In almost every case, yes. He is not prepared, and he remains sick for some time, very confused.

RON: Would you say something about the beneficial effects of hallucinogens, pills, as used today?

ULYSSES: I have already said it. You did not listen.

RON: Yes, you did. I'm sorry. I would like to ask one more question.

ULYSSES: Yes.

RON: If a person has, let us say, a particularly high incarnation, will he then possibly have a lower one the next time? And how does this go along with what you said about there being no going back, that it is a continual learning process, a development process? Is there just evolution in reincarnation, or is there also de-evolution?

ULYSSES: I understand. There must be all forms and a knowledge of all forms, so one may be high, a priest, and next he may be a ditchdigger, so that all may know all forms.

RON: Did you say that beings constantly come back to this Earth?

ULYSSES: The force returns to a being, yes.

RON: When a person passes on, does he recognize friends, relatives, and others whom he has known while he was here and who have gone on before him?

ULYSSES: If he has not been absorbed to the force and is in transition, as I am, yes.

RON: Do you have any general comments you might want to make to anyone in the group here?

ULYSSES: No.

The sessions were over. Ron and Carl have not returned to them. When I asked Ron why they didn't continue such absorbing and informative sessions, his answer was that what they had already received provided them all with grist for their thinking mill for a long time; and also, the immediate problems of personal, day-to-day survival were more pressing than going contemplative and dwelling overmuch on what is going to be in the hereafter. The sessions did provide, as Ron called it, soul food.

AFTERWORD

Most of the stories do not permit an implastic decision either for or against the hypothesis of reincarnation. Also, it is not enough to say flatly of the reincarnation theory, "I can't really see any sense in it," or "It's against all the rules." There is conformity in the memories of many of the stories to the psychological "law" that recognition exceeds recall, which places it in favor of the hypothesis.

With such a diversity in the narratives presented, hard and fast conclusions, except for personal ones, are hard to come by. Many coherent experiences or recollections of previous lives appear to occur in the forms of memories and as such do merit attention. Some of the people in the book have "seen" themselves in former lives, in other bodies, or have simply "known" the individuals they were seeing at the time they were themselves in different life situations.

At the present time we are still faced with the rule: If you believe, no explanation is necessary; if you don't believe, no explanation is possible. Argument for and against from either or both proponents of differing views are impossible to refute! By and large, concerning reincarnation, we are in the same arena with the person who states, "God spoke to me." The proposition can be abundant, the proof difficult.

Some possibly relevant concepts of reincarnative recollection are drawn through what is contained in hauntings, out-of-body experiences, communications from discarnates, materializations of the dead—the majority of such information purports to debouch from a personality whose body is dead but whose mind has survived and is allegedly functioning from another plane, another dimension invisible to the earth plane. The content of dreams, retrocognition, and regressive hypnosis supply other types of information which may or may not always be viable, though there is a considerable quantity of it.

We have seen that persons three or four years of age have had recollections or experiences; on the other hand so have adults of varying ages. The current tendency is to give more credence to the youngster who has reincarnative recollections, say to age eleven or twelve, and discredit those who have them beyond that age. But neither can be proved. What has been presented in other writings on reincarnation has whetted some academic and scientific appetites for a concerted, directed effort to be mounted in hopes of either proving it or discrediting it, but it seems likely that both attempts may remain without final, conclusive results.

It could be that in some of the stories there very possibly exists some hallucination or some cryptomnesia, i.e., fragmentary and incomplete recollection of something which happened in this life, attributed to a memory of a former life. We don't feel there has been out-and-out fraud by any of our relators. This book was written over a three year period during which we returned at varying intervals to all but two and had them recount their stories. Without prompting, it tallied in detail with what they had originally narrated on tape in the initial meetings when we obtained their stories.

The case for possession of a physically living human being by an excarnate, contained in the classic story of the Watseka Wonder, the case of Mary Roff and Lurancy Vennum, doesn't prove reincarnation but certainly provides substantial credence to the survival theory. We don't know what happens with personalities after death, but if it is a fact that they do survive, as it appears, it gives rise to the further hypothesis of the possibility of some kind of reincarnative experience that can be recalled when an individual comes into physical life, here on planet Earth, or elsewhere.

An interesting proposition is that of an excarnate personality evidencing through the medium of a living person without displacing the incumbent personality, of imparting the

Afterword

memory of their own former life to that individual in such a manner that the recipient feels he is experiencing recollections of that life as his own, since he has no other point of reference.

Throughout can be noted a correlation between what the relator said he experienced or remembered from a former life with incidents in this present life, recollections quite possibly from a previous life that correspond specifically with occurrences or patterns in this life.

Whether you believe reincarnation to be true or false, there is more compelling evidence for than against the theory; it weaves inexorably through the interstices of humankind, and throughout all of nature.

Some might admonish to "leave well enough alone," but we feel it is a concomitant accessory to the reincarnative hypothesis. It is *evolution,* as still hypothetical as reincarnation (although felt proven from time to time by various researchers). The first discussion concerns the diversity encountered within science and religion, which then extends and allows for what is considered by many as pretty bizarre reincarnative beliefs by some few individuals. There are pros and cons about reincarnation; there is the same about evolution.

Interviews with members of the science and religion fields indicate that a stand-off has developed between them regarding theories of evolution. Science has been more hardnosed than religion; actually, with a preponderance of what is considered irrefutable evidence and an overwhelming rhetoric, science has cowed religion into the compromise. That compromise has provided a cop-out for each: God created life through the process of organic *evolution.* This would solve the problem without a direct and on-going confrontation: (1) God is the first cause; (2) science provides the specific mechanisms by which His handiwork is carried into effect.

Additionally, this evolutionary hypothesis has paved the way for some individuals to adopt the view that since *every-*

thing evolved from the one primary source (God), it then follows that Man, reincarnatively, can return to life in any form (including Man), can live through animal, mineral, and vegetable life experiences. God started it all, and evolution carries out the effect. By God using evolutionary methods, He has contributed a common solution to what would otherwise be conflicting beliefs. A graphic example of the science–religion compromise is revealed by James H. Jaucey in *Science Returns To God*: "There are a great number of biologists who at least tentatively believe in evolution, but who nevertheless are active members of Christian churches and find no problem at all. The general attitude is that even if evolution were to prove true, instead of making God unnecessary, it would merely show that this was the method God used."

That God used a hit-or-miss evolutionary method is refuted from the biblical viewpoint if there is a strict adherence to a few verses in the Book of Genesis: "And God created great whales, and every living creature that moved, which the waters brought forth abundantly, *after their kind,* and every winged fowl *after his kind*: and God saw that it was good." (Gen. 1:21) Further on, "And God said, let the earth bring forth the living creature *after his kind,* cattle and creeping thing, and beast of the earth *after his kind.*" (Gen. 1:24) "And God made the beast of the earth *after his kind,* and cattle *after their kind,* and every thing that creepeth upon the earth *after his kind*: and God saw that it was good." (Gen. 1:25)

There doesn't appear to be any evolution "in the beginning." It does appear that life on this planet was variously created whole, and the variations have never crossed the biblical expression of that creation.

Observational science took a whack at interpretation when Carl O. Dunbar in *Historical Geology* wrote: "It is known for example, that all modern breeds of dog can be traced back to a single species of wild dog, that all our domestic horses

Afterword

have come from one or two species of wild pony, and that the many breeds of cattle have sprung from one, or at most a few, wild ancestors. If it has been possible, within a few thousand years, to change a wild dog into forms as diverse as the whippet, the bulldog, and the poodle, and if, by careful selection and breeding, it has been possible to transform the scrawny wild pony of central Asia into the sleek Arabian race horse, the toylike Shetland pony, and the ponderous Percheron, then we can only wonder if in similar fashion each kind of wild life has developed from some other, by gradual change and specialization. This line of thought led to the doctrine of Organic Evolution, which is the belief that from some geologically remote, primitive form of life all the diverse kinds of animals and plants have developed, each evolving from some previous form by gradual and orderly change. According to this conception, all creatures are genetically related, like the members of the great human family, and the degree of relationship of different groups of animals and plants may be represented by the branches of a family tree."

Obviously, geologist Dunbar has gone beyond the line of *observed* changes in life forms, beyond science, beyond accepted scripture, and he speculates in a most unscientific manner, waxing philosophic or assumptive in his conclusions. Each species of every thing can vary widely within its own kind, but it doesn't break out into other kinds. There have never been proven to be conclusive links between the *kinds*. It is well-known that early Man sexually coupled with beasts of the field, but mutations have never been known to evolve from those couplings, the *kind* remains within the kind, observably varying only a certain amount within that own life kind.

A theistic evolutionary acceptance places God in a rather untenable position of being weak, vacillating, capable of creating the spark of first life but then incapable of producing the more complex forms of life, which must find their own way by evolving. This is a denial of God's direct power. It can be aptly said that if a person adheres to the evolutionary thought, God is not present. If science and religion are joined in a step-one–step-two belief, each comes away with a poor compromise, at best.

BIBLIOGRAPHY

Cerminara, Gina. *Many Lives, Many Loves.* New York: Morrow, 1963.
Fodor, Nandor. *Encyclopaedia of Psychic Science.* New York: University Books, 1966.
Head, Joseph, and Cranston, S. L. *Reincarnation, an East–West Anthology.* Wheaton, Ill.: Theosophical Publishing House, 1968.
Myers, F. W. H. *Human Personality and Its Survival of Bodily Death.* New York: University Books, 1961.
Ostrander, Sheila, and Schroeder, Lynn. *Psychic Discoveries Behind the Iron Curtain.* Englewood Cliffs, N. J.: Prentice-Hall, 1970.
Roberts, Jane. *The Seth Material.* Englewood Cliffs, N. J.: Prentice-Hall, 1970.
Smith, Alson J. *Immortality.* New York: New American Library, 1967.
Spence, Lewis. *An Encyclopaedia of Occultism.* New York: University Books, 1968.
Steiger, Brad. *We Have Lived Before.* New York: Ace Books, 1967.
Stephenson, Ian. "Twenty Cases Suggestive of Reincarnation." In *Proceedings of the American Society for Psychical Research.* Vol. XXVI, 1966.
The Teachings of Silver Birch. London: Spiritualist Press, 1962.
Weatherhead, Leslie D. "The Case for Reincarnation." Lecture paper, City Temple Literary Society, 1957.

INDEX

Acupuncture, 54
Adams, C. L., 4–5
Adobe Walls, battle of, 149
Age regression, 163, 164, 165
Akashic records, 105, 107, 108, 120
Alcoholic beverages, 173–174
Alcoholism, 69
Alexander the Great, 11
Alexander, Jedidiah, 105, 106
American Indians, 13, 81–82, 84–87, 119, 146–150
Anaxagoras, 13
Anchor Cap and Closure Company, 39
Anthropology, 86, 154
Antony, Mark, 24
Apache Indians, 147
Apollonius, 13
Apparitions (Tyrell), 19
Arabian horses, 179
Archeology, 23, 153, 158
Aristotle, 13
Asch, Sholem, 13
Astral projecton, 76, 91–150, 171, 175
Astrology, 8–9, 13, 15, 19–20, 41–42, 52, 63–64, 75–76, 108
Augustine, Saint, 14
Aztec Indians, 82

Basuto Negro, 35
Bauder, Bob, 27
Bauder, Hazel, 27–31

Bendix, William, 40
Benik, Anthony, 91–109
Benik, Jan, 95, 96
Bible, 153, 161, 171–172, 178
Binning, George, 144–145
"Boomerang" reincarnation, 134
Bowie, Jim, 121–122
Bronchitis, 52
Buddhism, 13

Caesar, Julius, 13
Cahagnet, Ron and Sylvia, 59–60, 63
Campanella, Tommaso, 13
Cannibalism, 159
Canning, Willie, 141
Captain Midnight, 3, 32
Carson, Kit, 149–150
Castel Sant' Angelo (Rome), 64
Catherine the Great, 68
Cayce, Edgar, 91
Center for the Unexplained (Berkeley), 8
Chien Le Tsien, 102
Christianity, 24, 26, 170, 178
Cicero, 13
Cigarettes, 173
City College of New York, 32–33
Civil War, 105
Clairvoyance, 5, 15, 16–17, 109, 115, 140
Cleopatra, 23–24, 46
College of Cardinals, 87

Index

Columbia Broadcasting System (CBS), 3
Comanche Indians, 149
Confederate army, 105, 106
Continuing life, reincarnation and, 10, 123–129
Courtland, Ginnie, 112, 113, 114, 115
Cryptomnesia, 176
Crystal ball, 93

Da Vinci, Leonardo, 49, 50
Daniel Boone, 19
Darwin, Charles, 12
David, King, 26
Death Valley, 80–81
Deathbed observations, 18–22
"Deathbed Observations by Physicians and Nurses" (Osis), 18–19
Deathbed Visions (Barrett), 19
Déjà vu, 17, 31–36, 81
DeWolf, Billy, 163
Doland, Lucy, 111, 112–113
Doland, Monica, 110–115
Doland, Vickie, 114–115
Dostoevski, Fedor, 68
Dreaming true, 130–138
Dreams, 59–88, 176
  retrocognitive, 59
  sleeping, 14, 16, 18, 19, 27–31, 42–43, 61–63, 65–71, 72–73, 76–79, 80–82, 84, 121, 130–138
  waking, 14, 43–45, 46–47, 59, 72, 74, 79–80, 84, 86
  See also Hallucinations
Drugs, 173–174
Ducasse, C. J., 14
Dunbar, Carl O., 178–179
Dunn, Richard, 83–88

Egypt (ancient), 78

Eisenbud, Jules, 159
Elizabeth of Austria, 13
Empedocles, 13
English language, 68, 92, 97, 101, 104
Ephesus, ruins of, 23
Esoteric astrology, 75, 76
Evolution, 177–180
Exorcism, 60

Fichte, J. G., 13
Ford, Arthur, 11, 70
Frederick the Great, 13
French language, 29, 46
French Revolution, 46, 47

Gemini (zodiac sign), 39
Genesis, Book of, 178
Genghis Khan, 49, 50
George, Jack, 17
Gestalt therapy, 54
Gettysburg, battle of, 105
Glossalalia, 68, 171–172
Goethe, J. W. von, 13
Graham, Billy, 63
Great Ghosts of the West (Webb), 6, 45
Great Indian Desert, 158
Greece (ancient), 13
Gregory I, Pope, 87
Gurus, 98–99, 102

Hallucinations, 18, 19, 46, 97, 131, 156, 165, 176
  waking, 22–27
Hallucinogens, 174
Hawkens rifles, 149
Hawthorn Books, Incorporated, 7, 8
Hebrew language, 17
Hegel, G. W. F., 13
Heine, Heinrich, 13
Help Stamp Out Fair Play, 22

Index

Hilton Inn (Albuquerque), 147
Hinduism, 13
Historical Geology (Dunbar), 178–179
Hodgson, Richard, 144, 145
Hofbrau Restaurant (New York City), 37
Hogan, Kate, 141
Holden, Bill, 40
Holy Spirit, 171–172
Homosexuality, 67, 69
Human Personality and Its Survival of Bodily Death (Myers), 145
Hypnosis, 14, 141, 163–174, 176

Israel, Manasseh ben, 13

James, William, 19
Jaucey, James H., 178
Jesus Christ, 11, 13–14, 24, 25, 45, 108, 170–172
Jim Bowie, 122
Jochai, Simeon ben, 13
John (disciple), 24, 26
John the Baptist, 11
Judaism, 13, 14, 26
Judeus, Philo, 13

Kant, Immanuel, 13
Karma, 8, 15, 42
Koran, 161
Korean War, 96
Krause, Karl, 13
Kwahari Comanche Indians, 149

Ladd, Alan, 40
Lake, Veronica, 163
Lao-tzu, 12–13, 99
Latin language, 86
Leo I, Pope, 49, 50
Leo (zodiac sign), 111
Life reading, 48–56
  psychotherapy and, 54–56
Lithuanian language, 92

Lysergic acid diethylamide (LSD), 67

Macmillan Company, 6
Manson, Charles, 63
Marie Antoinette, 45
Masochism, 67
Mastoiditis, 52
Mediums, 4–5, 11, 15, 45–46, 48, 70, 102, 144, 170
  See also Psychics, Sensitives
Melton, Sidney, 3
Meningitis, 132
Mescalero Apache Indians, 147
Metempsychosis, 9, 59
Michelangelo, 13
Middleton, Robert, 22–27
Milland, Ray, 40, 163
Mohammedanism, 13, 24
Morris, Freda, 5, 6, 8, 12, 163
Moses, 11, 13
Mount Sinai, 26
Myers, F. W. H., 144, 145
Mystics, 13, 91
Mythology, 70

Napoleon I, 11, 45
Narcotics, 173
Nash Publishing Company, 5–6
Negroes, 31–36
Neptune (planet), 80
Neuropsychiatric Institute (University of California at Los Angeles), 5
New Testament, 171–172
New York Psychiatric Institute, 154
Newton, Isaac, 12
Neyland, James, 6–9
Nietzsche, Friedrich, 13
Nobel Prize, 71
Norwegian language, 68
Nuremberg trials, 154

Index

Oblath's Restaurant (Hollywood), 163
Ophthalmology, 113
Ophthalmovascularity, 113
Organic Evolution, doctrine of, 179
Osis, Karlis, 18–19
Ovid, 13

Paleobotany, 153
Paleontology, 153, 154, 158
Paleotropicism, 153
Palingenesis, 9
Paramount Studio, 40, 163
Parapsychology, 8, 75, 144, 145
Parapsychology Monograph, 19
Parker, Cynthia Ann, 149
Parker, Quanah, 149
"Peak in Darien" hypothesis, 19
Pedrarias Indians, 86
Phantasms, 18
Pizarro, Francisco, 84
Plato, 13, 17
Plotinus, 13
Plutarch, 13
Polo, Marco, 49
Pomona County Fair, 160
Precognition, 61, 72, 73, 114, 115
Preston, Bob, 163
Projection. *See* Astral projection
Prophecy and coincidence, pattern of, 3–15
Prostitution, 125
Protestants, 60
Psychiatry, 54–56, 66–67, 125, 153, 154, 157, 158, 160–161
Psychic magazine, 5, 6
Psychic recognition, 37–46
Psychics, 4, 42, 63, 76, 91, 92, 95, 108, 109, 111, 123–124
See also Mediums, Sensitives

Psychological warfare, 96
Psychology, 54–55, 76, 175
Psychometry, 6, 94–95, 104, 109
Psychotherapy, 54–56, 160
Pyramids, 79
Pythagoras, 13, 123

Rasputin, 68
Recall, types of, 16–37
  clairvoyant. *See* Clairvoyance
  deathbed observations, 18–22
  déjà vu, 17, 31–36
  in sleeping dreams, 16, 18, 27–31
  theories for, 18
  waking hallucinations, 22–27
Reich, Wilhelm, 54
Reincarnation
  "boomerang," 134
  clairvoyance and. *See* Clairvoyance
  concept in children, 16–17, 176
  and continuing life, 10, 123–129
  defined, 9–10
  dreams as evidence for, 59–88
  numbers of believers, 12–14
  problem of proving, 59
  Roman Catholic Church on, 13–14
  test of belief in, 11–12
  numbers of believers, 12–14
Religio-Philosophical Journal, The, 144
Resurrection, physical, 171
Retrocognition, 59, 115, 176
Richter, J. P. F., 13
Roman Catholic Church, 13–14, 46, 91, 93, 170
Rome (ancient), 13, 51
Roff, Mary, 139–145, 176
Roff, Minerva, 142

Index

Russell, Gail, 163

Saint Francis of Assisi, 14
Sallust, 13
San Blas Indians, 86
Sanskrit, 104–105
Schlegel, Friedrich von, 13
Schopenhauer, Arthur, 13
Schweitzer, Albert, 13
Science Returns to God (Jaucey), 178
Scorpio (zodiac sign), 63
Seance, 48
Search for the Girl with the Green Eyes, The (Stearn), 75
Sensitives, 4, 6, 7
 See also Mediums, Psychics
Serios, Ted, 159
Sexual intercourse, 157, 161, 170–171, 179
Sharps Breechloading Percussion Single-shot Carbine, 149–150
Shetland ponies, 160, 179
Sinusitis, 52
Slaves, 31–36, 51
Smallpox, 35
Solomon, King, 13
Southern California Society for Psychical Research, 5, 153
Spirit communication, 163–174
Stearn, Jess, 75
Steiner, Rudolf, 13
Stevens, E. W., 140, 141, 143, 144, 145
Stevenson, Ian, 14
Stigmata, 6
Suffocation, 63–64
Suicide, 9, 41
Swastika patterns, 82
Swedish language, 68
Synchronicity, 3, 8

Talmud, 161
Taoism, 13
Telekinesis, 95, 112, 115
Telepathy, 122
Theosophists, 13
Tiffen, Gregge, 48–56
Time-tripping, 91–150
Tolstoi, Leo, 68
Tongues, speaking in, 68, 171–172
Total recall memory, 92
Trances, 11, 79, 126, 144, 145, 153–162
Transference, 114
Transfiguration, 68–70
Transitional lifetimes, 65–71
Transmigration, 9, 59
Tsai Mei Lamasery, 99–105, 107
"Twenty Cases Suggestive of Reincarnation" (Stevenson), 14
Tyrell, G. N. M., 19

U.S. Army, 39
U.S. Navy, 95
Universal Christ Church, 109
University of California at Los Angeles, 6
University of Southern California, 158

Varieties of Religious Experience (James), 19
Vaughan, Alan, 6–7, 9
Vennum, Lurancy, 139–145, 176
Virgil, 13
Virgin Mary, 11, 24, 25, 26, 127
Vital, Chajim, 13

Wagner, Richard, 13
Warner Brothers, 3

Webb, Clifton, 6
Webb, Florence, 8, 9, 19–20, 38–46, 65, 69–70, 118
Webster's New Twentieth Century Dictionary, 9–10
World War II, 40, 154

Xenoglossis, 172

Yosemite National Park, 80

Zodiac signs, 39, 63, 111
Zoroastrianism, 13